INTERWEAVE
PRESENTS

knitted gifts

Irresistible Projects
to Make & Give

INTERWEAVE.
interweavestore.com

COVER & INTERIOR DESIGN
pamela norman

PHOTOGRAPHY
joe hancock, unless otherwise noted

PHOTO STYLING
pamela chavez

WARDROBE STYLING/HAIR & MAKEUP
carol beaver

TECHNICAL EDITOR
jean lampe

ILLUSTRATIONS
gayle ford

PRODUCTION DESIGN
katherine jackson

Projects © 2009 Individual designers
Photography © 2009 Joe Hancock, unless otherwise noted
Illustrations © 2009 Interweave Press LLC

Interweave Press LLC
201 East Fourth Street
Loveland, CO 80537-5655 USA
Interweavestore.com

Printed in China by Asia Pacific Offset

Library of Congress Cataloging-in-Publication Data
Budd, Ann, 1956-
    Interweave presents knitted gifts : irresistible
projects to make and give / Ann Budd, author.
      p. cm.
  Includes index.
  ISBN 978-1-59668-091-3 (pbk.)
  1. Knitting--Patterns. I. Interweave Press. II. Title.
  TT820.B7865 2009
  746.43'2043--dc22
                       2009002918

10 9 8 7 6 5 4 3 2 1

acknowledgments

This book is dedicated to everyone who has given or received a handknitted gift. In particular, thanks go to the talented designers who came up with the ideas and knitted them into realities for this book: Pam Allen, Véronik Avery, Nancy Bush, Gregory Courtney, Chrissy Gardiner, Kim Hamlin, Therese Inverso, Mags Kandis, Cecily Glowik MacDonald, Marta McCall, Kathy Merrick, Kristin Nicholas, Ruthie Nussbaum, Vicki Square, Jaya Srikrishnan, Elissa Sugishita, Judith L. Swartz, Kathy Ticho, JoLene Treace, and last but never least, Kathy Zimmerman.

The projects in this book were made possible in part by yarn donated by a number of generous manufacturers: Blue Sky Alpacas, Brown Sheep Company, Caron International, Classic Elite Yarns, Crystal Palace Yarns, Dale of Norway, DMC, Universal Yarns, Fiesta Yarns, T&C Imports, Lily, Lorna's Laces, Louet North America, Morehouse Farm, Muench Yarns, Plymouth Yarn Company, Schoolhouse Press, Tahki/Stacy Charles, Toots LeBlanc and Company, Trendsetter Yarns, Tutto Santa Fe, and Westminster Fibers.

Tricia Waddell, Rebecca Campbell, and Pamela Norman of Interweave offered encouragement, advice, and valuable expertise. Carol Beaver and Pam Chavez helped style the photographs, and Joe Hancock brought them to life with his mastery of light and film.

And finally, to my family and my best knitting gal-pals—Carmen, Darcy, Jane, Judy, Stephanie, and Susan—for constant inspiration in the spirit of gift giving.

ann budd ✿

contents

the gift of giving

Like most children, I was taught "it is better to give than receive." While I struggled with this adage as a young girl, I came to embrace the wisdom as I matured, especially when I learned to knit. There are few things that give me as much pleasure as feeling yarn travel through my fingers in a rhythmic pulse as stitches form one by one. I simply love to knit. So it's no wonder that I get double (albeit selfish) pleasure out of knitting gifts for friends and family. I get to choose beautiful yarn—sometimes luxury yarn that I wouldn't buy for myself—and try out stitch patterns, color combinations, and techniques that I might otherwise overlook. Left unchecked, my closets, drawers, nooks, and crannies would overflow with more knitted sweaters, scarves, hats, and socks than I could possibly wear. But by giving my handknits as gifts, I can always justify buying more yarn and abandoning the housework to knit for hours—it's for someone else, not me, I rationalize. And then, there's the moment when the happy recipient gushes over the fact that I took time to create a one-of-a-kind gift and recognizes the tiny bit of me that's in every stitch. There's no doubt that I come out on top.

For *Knitted Gifts*, I asked other knitters, many of them accomplished designers, to come up with unusual and inspired projects that they would like to give (or receive) as gifts. Thirty-two of their best ideas are compiled in this book. Whether you're looking for a quick one-skein scarf or an heirloom-quality baby blanket, you'll find lots of choices to delight everyone on your gift list— men, women, and children. But don't resist the temptation to make something just for you along the way. There's plenty of joy to be had in giving a gift to yourself, too!

herringbone
SCARF

Don't have a lot of time? Don't worry—you can knit up **Gregory Courtney's** little scarf in a snap. Just knit two halves from the front to the center back (the yarn is used double for quicker knitting), then join them together with a three-needle bind-off, and you're done. The decorative edge, created along the way with slipped stitches at each end of the needle, provides stability so the scarf won't stretch in length. Each scarf requires just one skein of yarn.

FINISHED SIZE About 3" (7.5 cm) wide at base and 40" (101.5 cm) long.

YARN Fingering weight (#1 Super Fine), used double. *Shown here:* Isager Alpaca 2 (50% alpaca, 50% wool; 275 yd [251 m]/50 g): 1 skein. Shown in #017 brass and #018 light olive.

NEEDLES Size U.S. 6 (4 mm). Adjust needle size if necessary to obtain the correct gauge.

NOTIONS Stitch holder; tapestry needle.

GAUGE 30 stitches and 30 rows = 4" (10 cm) in pattern stitch with two strands of yarn held together.

Row 6 Sl 1 kwise wyb, sl 1 pwise wyf, p1, k2, p6, k1, p6, k2, sl 1 pwise wyf, p1tbl, p1.

Rep these 6 rows 4 more times—piece measures about 4" (10 cm) from CO.

Decrease for Strap

Dec row: (RS) [Sl 1 kwise wyb] 2 times, k1, ssk, knit to last 5 sts, k2tog, sl 1 pwise wyb, k1, p1—2 sts dec'd; 21 sts rem.

Next row: (WS) Sl 1 kwise wyb, sl 1 pwise wyf, p1, purl to last 3 sts, sl 1 pwise wyf, p1tbl, p1.

Rep the last 2 rows 3 more times, ending with a WS row—15 sts rem.

Strap

With RS facing, [sl 1 kwise wyb] 2 times, k1, knit to last 3 sts, sl 1 pwise wyb, k1, p1.

Next row (WS) Sl 1 kwise wyb, sl 1 pwise wyf, p1, knit to last 3 sts, sl 1 pwise wyf, p1tbl, p1.

Rep the last 2 rows until piece measures about 20" (51 cm) from CO edge, ending with a WS row. Place sts on holder.

Make another piece to match, but leave the sts on needle.

FINISHING

Place held 15 sts of first half on empty needle. Hold the two pieces with RS facing tog and WS facing out. Use the three-needle method (see *Glossary*) to BO the sts tog.

Weave in loose ends. Block gently.

SCARF HALF (make 2)

With two strands of yarn held tog, CO 23 sts.

Set-up row (WS) Sl 1 kwise with yarn in back (wyb), sl 1 pwise with yarn in front (wyf), p1, k2, p6, k1, p6, k2, sl 1 pwise wyf, p1 through back loop (p1tbl), p1.

Row 1 (RS) [Sl 1 kwise wyb] 2 times, k1, p2, M1L (see *Glossary*), k3, p2, p3tog, p2, k3, M1R (see *Glossary*), p2, sl 1 pwise wyb, k1, p1.

Row 2 (WS) Sl 1 kwise wyb, sl 1 pwise wyf, p1, k2, p4, k5, p4, k2, sl 1 pwise wyf, p1tbl, p1.

Row 3 [Sl 1 kwise wyb] 2 times, k1, p2, M1L, k4, p1, p3tog, p1, k4, M1R, p2, sl 1 pwise wyb, k1, p1.

Row 4 Sl 1 kwise wyb, sl 1 pwise wyf, p1, k2, p5, k3, p5, k2, sl 1 pwise wyf, p1tbl, p1.

Row 5 [Sl 1 kwise wyb] 2 times, k1, p2, M1L, k5, p3tog, k5, M1R, p2, sl 1 pwise wyb, k1, p1.

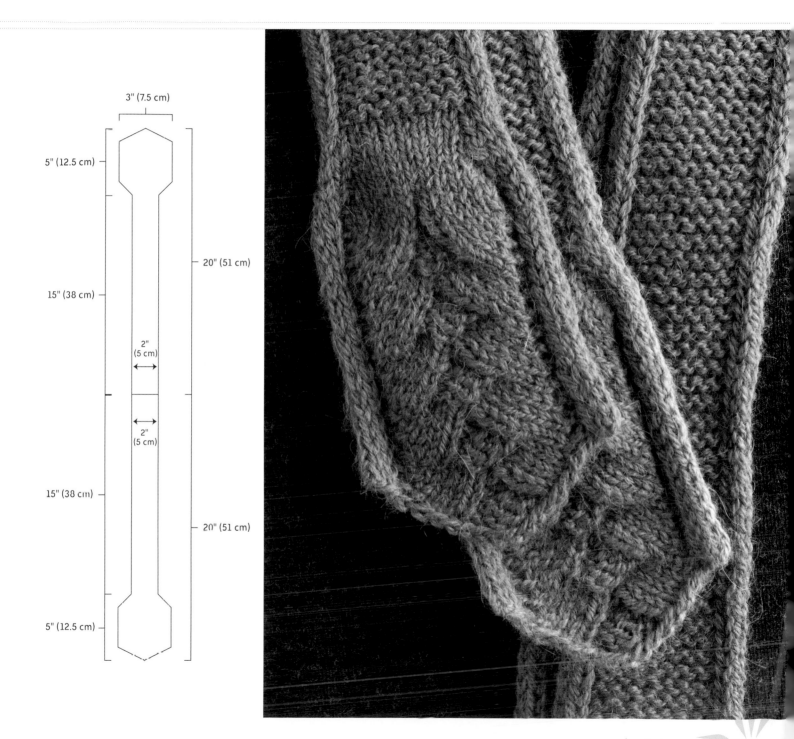

3" (7.5 cm)

5" (12.5 cm)

20" (51 cm)

15" (38 cm)

2" (5 cm)

2" (5 cm)

15" (38 cm)

20" (51 cm)

5" (12.5 cm)

folded tweed
BAG

*A*fter seeing a bag constructed out of folded leather in an upscale shop in Milan, **Kathy Merrick** was intrigued by the idea of folding knitted fabric to create a similar look. This striped tweed version begins as a simple rectangle. A mitered garter-stitch edging is added around all four sides, then the fabric is folded to form a pleat at the center top and each lower corner to give it shape. Two lengths of I-cord form the handle and larger decorative buttons complete the rustic look.

FINISHED SIZE About 24½" (62 cm) wide and 26½" (67.5 cm) long, including edging, before folding.

YARN Worsted weight (#4 Medium).
Shown here: Plymouth Yarns Plymouth Tweed (100% wool; 109 yd [98 m]/50 g): #5313 rust (MC), 3 skeins; #5315 burgundy (A), 2 skeins; #5328 pink (B) and #5320 deep purple (C), 1 skein each.

NEEDLES *Bag:* size U.S. 7 (4.5 mm): 32" (80 cm) cir (circular). *I-cord:* size U.S. 6 (4 mm): set of 2 double-point (dpn). Adjust needle size if necessary to obtain the correct gauge.

NOTIONS Markers (m); tapestry needle; sharp-point sewing needle and matching thread; four 2" (5 cm) buttons; ¾ yd (70 cm) lightweight woven cotton for lining, straight pins.

GAUGE 17 stitches and 28 rows = 4" (10 cm) in stockinette stitch.

[2 rows A, 2 rows MC] 3 times.

2 rows A.

8 rows MC.

[2 rows C, 2 rows MC] 3 times.

2 rows C.

Rep from * once.

8 rows MC.

[2 rows B, 2 rows MC] 3 times.

2 rows B.

8 rows MC—piece measures about 23" (58.5 cm) from CO.

Edging

Work edging in garter st in the rnd as foll: With A, k1, M1 (see Glossary), k98, M1, place marker (pm), k1, pick up and knit 102 sts along left edge as foll: *pick up and knit 1 st for each of the next 2 rows, skip 1 row, pick up and knit 1 st for each of the next 3 rows, skip 1 row; rep from * to end of left edge, pm, pick up and knit first CO loop, M1, pick up and knit in each of the next 98 CO loops, M1, pm, pick up and knit last CO loop, pick up and knit 102 sts along right edge as for left edge, pm—408 sts total. Purl 1 rnd.

Inc rnd: Knit and *at the same time* *M1 before marker, slip marker, knit 1, M1; rep from * at each marker—8 sts inc'd.

Rep the last 2 rnds 4 more times—448 sts total. BO all sts.

FINISHING

Gently steam-press bag body to block. Weave in loose ends.

With A threaded on a tapestry needle, RS facing, and using the fishbone st (see Glossary), sew seam.

Lining

Cut lining to fit striped portion of the bag (do not line the edging), plus 1" (2.5 cm) for seam allowance. Press lining edge under ½" (1.3 cm) on each side. With sharp-point sewing needle and matching thread, sew lining to first garter ridge of edging.

BAG BODY

With MC and cir needle, CO 100 sts. Work in St st (knit RS rows; purl WS rows) in the foll stripe sequence:

*8 rows MC.

[2 rows B, 2 rows MC] 3 times.

2 rows B.

8 rows MC.

Handles

With MC and dpn, CO 6 sts. Work 6-st I-cord (see Glossary) until piece measures 24" (61 cm) from CO. BO all sts. With A, make another cord the same. Tie the two cords tog in a square knot at the center and 2½" (6 cm) from each end.

Assembly

Fold a 2½" (6 cm) pleat at the center of each long side to shape the top of the bag. With sewing needle and thread, sew a button through all layers at the top of each pleat (**Figure 1**). Fold bag in half from lengthwise and with A threaded on a tapestry needle, sew front and back tog at the upper corners. Sandwich each sewn-together corner between the ends of the two handle cords and sew through all layers securely. Fold a 2½" (6.5 cm) pleat at each lower corner and sew a button through all layers (**Figure 2**).

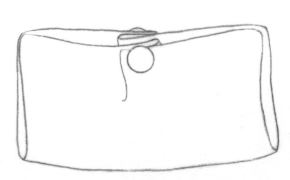

Figure 1

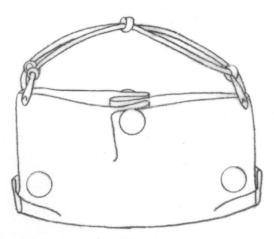

Figure 2

hourglass
RIB SOCKS

*T*he waving cable pattern in **Chrissy Gardiner's** ribbed socks looks like stacked hourglasses or repeating Xs and Os. Either way you look at it, it makes a great pair of socks. Chrissy chose an alpaca-blend yarn that has a bit of a halo to soften the pattern while adding a luxurious feel. The socks are worked from the top down to the toe, with the ribbed pattern extending along the instep for a comfortable fit.

FINISHED SIZE About 7½" (9, 10½)" (19 [24, 28] cm) foot circumference, 8½ (10, 11)" (21.5 [25.5, 28] cm) foot length from back of heel to tip of toe, and 6 (7, 8)" (15 [18, 20.5] cm) leg length. Socks shown measure 7½" (19 cm) foot circumference.

YARN Fingering weight (#1 Super Fine).
Shown here: Classic Elite Alpaca Sox (60% alpaca, 20% merino wool, 20% nylon; 450 yd [411 m]/100 g): #1825 russet, 1 (1, 2) skein(s).

NEEDLES Size U.S. 1 (2.25 mm): set of 5 double-pointed (dpn). Adjust needle size if necessary to obtain the correct gauge.

NOTIONS Cable needle (cn); tapestry needle.

GAUGE 16 stitches and 20 rounds = 2" (5 cm) in stockinette stitch, worked in rounds.

stitch guide

+ C2F (worked over 2 sts)
Slip 1 st onto cable needle and hold in front, k1,
k1 from cable needle.
+ C2B (worked over 2 sts)
Slip 1 st onto cable needle and hold in back,
k1, k1 from cable needle.

LEG

CO 66 (78, 90) sts. Arrange sts so there are 16 (19, 22) sts
on Needle 1, 17 (20, 23) sts on Needle 2, 17 (20, 23) sts
on Needle 3, and 16 (19, 22) sts on Needle 4. Join sts for
working in rnds, being careful not to twist sts—rnd begins
at center of back leg; back-of-leg and bottom-of-foot sts are
divided between Needles 1 and 4; front-of-leg and instep
sts are divided between Needles 2 and 3.

Rnds 1 and 2 K2, *p2 (3, 4), k3, p2 (3, 4), k4; rep from * to
last 9 (11, 13) sts, p2 (3, 4), k3, p2 (3, 4), k2.

Rnd 3 C2B (see *Stitch Guide*), *p2 (3, 4), k3, p2 (3, 4), C2F
(see *Stitch Guide*), C2B; rep from * to last 9 (11, 13) sts,
p2 (3, 4) k3, p2 (3, 4), C2F.

Rnds 4, 5, 6 Rep Rnd 1.

Rnd 7 C2F, *p2 (3, 4), k3, p2 (3, 4), C2B, C2F; rep from * to
last 9 (11, 13) sts, p2 (3, 4), k3, p2 (3, 4), C2B.

Rnd 8 Rep Rnd 1.

Rep Rnds 1–8 until leg measures about 6 (7, 8)" (15 [18,
20.5] cm) from CO or desired length to top of heel flap,
ending with Needle 3 completed on Rnd 4 or 8 of patt.

HEEL

Slip 16 (19, 22) sts from Needle 4 onto Needle 1—32 (38,
44) heel sts on one needle; rem 34 (40, 46) instep sts will
be worked later when the gussets are picked up.

Heel Flap

Work 32 (38, 44) heel sts back and forth in rows as foll:

Row 1: (RS) *Sl 1 pwise with yarn in back (wyb), k1; rep
from *.

Row 2 (WS) Sl 1 pwise with yarn in front (wyf), purl to end.
Rep Rows 1 and 2 until heel flap measures 2 (3, 3½)" (5
[7.5, 9] cm) or desired length from beg of flap. (**Note** Try on
the sock to make sure the flap reaches the base of the heel
when the heel touches the ground.)

Turn Heel

Work short-rows as foll:

Row 1 (RS) Sl 1 pwise wyb, k16 (20, 24), ssk, k1, turn work.

Row 2 (WS) Sl 1 pwise wyf, p3 (5, 7), p2tog, p1, turn.

Row 3 Sl 1 pwise wyb, knit to 1 st before gap, ssk (1 st each
side of gap), k1, turn.

Row 4 Sl 1 pwise wyf, purl to 1 st before gap, p2tog (1 st
each side of gap), p1, turn.

Rep Rows 3 and 4 until all heel sts have been worked—18
(22, 26) heel sts rem.

Gussets

Pick up sts along selvedge edges of heel flap and rejoin for
working in rnds as foll:

Rnd 1 On Needle 1, K9 (11, 13) to half-way point of heel
sts, place marker to denote beg of rnd, k9 (11, 13)
rem heel sts, pick up and knit 16 (22, 25) sts along
selvedge edge of heel flap; on Needles 2 and 3, work
in established patt across 34 (40, 46) instep sts; with
empty Needle 4, pick up and knit 16 (22, 25) sts along
other selvedge edge of heel flap, then k9 (11, 13) from
Needle 1 to marker—84 (106, 122) sts total.

Note Gusset decreases are worked at the end of Needle
1 and the beg of Needle 4 only.

Rnd 2 On Needle 1, knit; on Needles 2 and 3, work in
established patt across instep sts; on Needle 4, knit to
end of rnd.

Rnd 3 On Needle 1, knit to last 3 sts, k2tog, k1; on Needles
2 and 3, work in established patt; on Needle 4, k1, ssk,
knit to end of rnd—2 sts dec'd.

Rep Rnds 2 and 3 until 68 (80, 92) sts rem—17 (20, 23) sts
on each needle.

FOOT

Working instep sts (Needles 2 and 3) in patt and bottom-of-foot sts (Needles 1 and 4) in St st, cont as established until piece measures about 6½ (7½, 8¼)" (16.5 [19, 21] cm) from back of heel, or about 2 (2½, 2¾)" (5 [6.5, 7] cm) less than desired finished length.

TOE

Dec at each side of foot as foll:

Rnd 1 On Needle 1, knit to last 3 sts, k2tog, k1; on Needle 2, k1, ssk, knit to end of needle; on Needle 3, knit to last 3 sts, k2tog, k1; on Needle 4, k1, ssk, knit to end of rnd—4 sts dec'd.

Rnd 2 Knit.

Rep Rnds 1 and 2 until 40 (44, 52) sts rem, then rep Rnd 1 only (i.e., dec every rnd) until 16 (20, 20) sts rem.

FINISHING

Knit the 4 (5, 5) sts from Needle 1 onto Needle 4 and slip the 4 (5, 5) sts from Needle 3 onto Needle 2—8 (10, 10) sts each on 2 needles. Cut yarn leaving a 12" (30.5 cm) tail. Thread tail on a tapestry needle and use the Kitchener st (see Glossary) to graft live sts tog. Weave in loose ends. Dampen socks and lay flat or place on sock blockers to block.

fair isle
PILLOW

*K*ristin Nicholas's richly colored pillow is a study in positive and negative, with the dominant colors reversing with each pattern band. Contrasting stripes of reverse stockinette stitch, a bit of duplicate stitch, and plenty of French knots add to the fun. Kristin worked the pillow top back and forth in rows, then picked up stitches around the four edges and worked the border in colorful reverse-stockinette stitch in rounds. She backed the pillow with a coordinating piece of silk fabric.

FINISHED SIZE About 16" (40.5 cm) square.

YARN Worsted weight (#4 Medium).
Shown here: Nashua Handknits Julia (50% wool, 25% alpaca, 25% mohair; 93 yd [85 m]/50 g): #NHJ2163 golden honey (A), #NHJ0178 harvest spice (B), #NHJ6396 deep blue sea (C), #NHJ3961 lady's mantle (D), and #NHJ3158 purple basil (E), 1 skein each.

NEEDLES *Pillow top:* sizes U.S. 5 and 7 (3.75 and 4.5 mm): straight. *Edging:* size U.S. 5 (3.75 mm): 32" (80 cm) circular (cir). Adjust needle size if necessary to obtain the correct gauge.

NOTIONS 4 markers (m), one of a unique color; tapestry needle; ½ yd (.5 meter) backing fabric; 16" (40.5 cm) pillow form; sharp-point sewing needle and matching thread.

GAUGE 20 stitches and 22 rows = 4" (10 cm) in colorwork pattern on larger needles or in single-color stockinette stitch on smaller needles.

NOTE
+ Use smaller needles for single-color rows; use larger needles for two-color rows.

stitch guide

**+ REVERSE STOCKINETTE STITCH RIDGE
  WORKED IN ROWS (beg with RS row)**
Row 1 (RS) Knit.
Row 2 Knit.
Row 3 Purl.

**+ REVERSE STOCKINETTE STITCH RIDGE
  WORKED IN ROWS (beg with WS row)**
Row 1 (WS) Purl.
Row 2 Purl.
Row 3 Knit.

**+ REVERSE STOCKINETTE STITCH RIDGE
  WORKED IN ROUNDS**
Rnd 1 (RS) Knit.
Rnds 2 and 3 (RS) Purl.

PILLOW TOP

With A and smaller needles, CO 72 sts. Beg with a WS row, work Rows 1–60 of Pillow chart, then work Rows 1–24 once more (84 rows total), always changing to larger needles for rows that involve two-colors and changing to smaller needles for single-color stripes. With A, BO all sts. **Note** Additional colors will be duplicate stitched in place later.

Border (worked in rounds)

With E, cir needle, and RS facing, *pick up and knit 70 sts along CO edge (do not include first and last sts), place marker (pm), pick up and knit 1 st in corner, pm, pick up and knit 64 sts evenly spaced along selvedge edge (pick up 1 st for every 3 of 4 rows), pm, pick up 1 st in corner, pm, pick up and knit 70 sts along BO edge (do not include first and last sts), pm, pick up and knit 1 st in corner, pm, pick up and knit 64 sts evenly spaced along other selvedge edge, pm, pick up and knit 1 st in corner—272 sts total. Pm of unique color and join for working in rnds. With E, work as foll: *Purl to m, M1 (see Glossary), slip marker (sl m), k1 (corner st), M1; rep from * to end of rnd—280 sts. Purl 1 rnd, knitting each corner st. Change to D and work reverse stockinette ridge worked in rnds (see Stitch Guide), inc 2

sts at each corner on Rnds 1 and 3—296 sts after Rnd 3 of patt. Change to C and work 3 rnds of reverse stockinette ridge, inc 2 sts at each corner on Rnd 2—304 sts. With C, firmly BO all sts purlwise.

FINISHING

Weave in loose ends.

Embroidery

With E or C threaded on a tapestry needle, work a duplicate st (see Glossary) in the center of each motif as shown in the photo, alternating colors. With 2 strands of E or C threaded on a tapestry needle, work French knots (see Glossary) at each outside corner of the embroidered center, using the opposite color than used for the center. With two strands of E, skip 1 or 2 sts, then work French knots evenly spaced along the C (blue) side of the rev St st stripes. With two strands of C, work French knots evenly spaced along the D (green) side of the rev St st stripes. Work French knots all the way around the outside edge, just inside the border.

Blocking

Using a spray bottle, thoroughly mist the pillow top with warm water. Work the water into the knitted fabric with your hands. Pin the fabric on flat padded surface (the top of a bed works well). Hold a steam iron 2" (5 cm) above the top of the fabric and steam lightly, being careful not to touch the iron to the fabric. Allow to air-dry thoroughly. (Alternately, handwash the pillow top in cold water with a cold rinse and lay it flat to dry.)

Assembly

Cut the backing fabric 1" (2.5 cm) wider and longer than the blocked pillow top. Turn under ½" (1.3 cm) seam allowance on all four sides and press. With sharp-point sewing needle, matching thread, and RS facing tog, handstitch the pillow top to three sides of the backing fabric. Insert the pillow form. Sew the fourth side.

Pillow

knit on RS; purl on WS
unless otherwise indicated

⊠	color A—golden honey
◈	color B—harvest spice
▲	color C—deep blue sea
▲	color C—purl on RS; knit on WS
‖	color D—lady's mantle
‖	color D—purl on RS; knit on WS
▣	color E—purple basil
▪	color E—purl on RS; knit on WS
☐	pattern repeat

Work 16 sts between markers 3 times

Note Chart begins with a wrong-side row.

curry & spice
HAT & SCARF

For this hat and scarf set, **Kathy Zimmerman** used a quick and easy variation of the blackberry stitch in a soft and inviting self-striping yarn. The stitch pattern involves complementary increases and decreases that result in a non-curling textured fabric that looks good on both sides—just right for a simple scarf. The matching hat is worked back and forth in rows and seamed along the center back.

FINISHED SIZE *Hat:* About 17½ (19½, 22)" (44.5 [49.5, 56] cm) head circumference, after blocking. To fit a toddler (child, adult). Hat shown in adult size.

Scarf: About 4 (6½)" (10 [16.5] cm) wide and 44 (60)" (112 [152.5] cm) long, after blocking. To fit a child (adult). Scarf shown in adult size.

YARN Chunky weight (#5 Bulky). *Shown here:* Crystal Palace Merino Stripes (90% merino, 10% acrylic; 115 yd [106 m]/50 g): #27 curry & spice, 1 ball for hat (all sizes); 1 (2) ball(s) for scarf.

NEEDLES *Scarf and hat body:* size 10½ (6.5 mm): straight. *Hat edging:* size 10 (6 mm): straight. Adjust needle size if necessary to obtain the correct gauge.

NOTIONS Tapestry needle.

GAUGE 11 stitches and 16 rows = 4" (10 cm) in textured pattern stitch on larger needles, slightly stretched after blocking.

stitch guide

+ TEXTURED PATTERN STITCH (multiple of 2 sts)
Note *The stitch count varies after Rows 2, 3, 6, and 7; count stitches only after Rows 1, 4, 5, or 8.*
Row 1 (RS) Purl.
Row 2 *K1, (k1, p1, k1) in next st; rep from *—patt is now a multiple of 4 sts.
Row 3 *K3, p1; rep from *.
Row 4 *K1, p3tog; rep from *—patt is now a multiple of 2 sts.
Row 5 Purl.
Row 6 *(K1, p1, k1) in next st, k1; rep from *—patt is now a multiple of 4 sts.
Row 7 *P1, k3; rep from *.
Row 8 *P3tog, k1; rep from *—patt is now a multiple of 2 sts.
Repeat Rows 1–8 for pattern.

HAT

With smaller needles, CO 53 (59, 65) sts. Knit 5 rows, inc 1 st at end of last row—54 (60, 66) sts. Change to larger needles and work in textured pattern until piece measures about 4 (5, 6)" (10 [12.5, 15] cm) from CO, ending with WS Row 4 or 8 of patt.

Shape Crown

Row 1 *K4, k2tog; rep from *—45 (50, 55) sts rem.
Row 2 and all WS rows Purl.
Row 3 *K3, k2tog; rep from *— 36 (40, 44) sts rem.
Row 5 *K2, k2tog; rep from *— 27 (30, 33) sts rem.
Row 7 *K1, k2tog; rep from *—18 (20, 22) sts rem.
Row 9 *K2tog; rep from *—9 (10, 11) sts rem.

FINISHING

Cut yarn, leaving a 6" (15 cm) tail. Thread tail on a tapestry needle and draw it through rem sts, pull tight to close top, and sew sides tog. Weave in loose ends.

SCARF

With larger needles, CO 10 (16) sts. Knit 5 rows. Work in textured pattern until piece measures 43 (59)" (109 [150] cm) from CO, ending with Row 1 of patt. Knit 5 rows. BO all sts.

FINISHING

Weave in loose ends. Block lightly to measurements.

QUICK COASTERS

Vivian Høxbro has filled two books (*Domino Knitting* and *Knit to be Square,* published by Interweave in 2002 and 2008, respectively) with ways to combine mitered squares into an artful array of garments and accessories. Used individually, a simple variation of Vivian's mitered-square technique makes pretty nifty coasters, too. These coasters are made from yarn leftover from Kathy Merrick's Folded Tweed Bag (page 12). Add stripes (always changing colors on right-side rows) and combine different yarns for variation.

CO 31 sts. Knit 1 (WS) row.
Row 1 (RS) K14, sl 2 tog kwise, k1, p2sso, k14—29 sts rem.
Row 2 and all even- numbered rows (WS) Knit.
Row 3 K13, sl 2 tog kwise, k1, p2sso, k13—27 sts rem.
Row 5 K12, sl 2 tog kwise, k1, p2sso, k12—25 sts rem.
Row 7 K11, sl 2 tog kwise, k1, p2sso, k11—23 sts rem.
Row 9 K10, sl 2 tog kwise, k1, p2sso, k10—21 sts rem.
Row 11 K9, sl 2 tog kwise, k1, p2sso, k9—19 sts rem.
Row 13 K8, sl 2 tog kwise, k1, p2sso, k8—17 sts rem.
Row 15 K7, sl 2 tog kwise, k1, p2sso, k7—15 sts rem.
Row 17 K6, sl 2 tog kwise, k1, p2sso, k6—13 sts rem.
Row 19 K5, sl 2 tog kwise, k1, p2sso, k5—11 sts rem.
Row 21 K4, sl 2 tog kwise, k1, p2sso, k4—9 sts rem.
Row 23 K3, sl 2 tog kwise, k1, p2sso, k3—7 sts rem.
Row 25 K2, sl 2 tog kwise, k1, p2sso, k2—5 sts rem.
Row 27 K1, sl 2 tog kwise, k1, p2sso, k1—3 sts rem.
Row 29 Sl 2 tog kwise, k1, p2sso—1 st rem.
Cut yarn and pull tail through rem loop to secure. Weave in loose ends. Submerge in water, blot with towels, pull into shape, and allow to air-dry thoroughly.

FINISHED SIZE About 3" (7.5 cm) square.

YARN Worsted weight (#4 Medium). *Shown here:* Plymouth Yarns Plymouth Tweed (100% wool; 109 yd [98 m]/50 g): about 8 yds for each coaster. Shown in #5313 rust, #5315 burgundy, and #5320 deep purple.

NEEDLES Size U.S. 7 (4.5 mm).

NOTIONS Tapestry needle.

GAUGE 10 stitches and 20 rows = 2" (5 cm) in garter stitch. Exact gauge is not critical but will affect final dimensions.

hobby
HORSE

*T*his hobby horse is modeled after one I made as a schoolgirl in 1969 as a lesson in sock knitting. The version I made back then was knitted with cotton yarn and the textured patterns were covered with duplicate stitch. Happily, the stitches in this felted version are too obscured for duplicate stitch—they are worked in accent colors instead. Simply knit a large sock out of wool yarn, felt it in the washing machine, add a few details, stuff it with fiberfill, and you've got a gift to keep your lil' cowpoke happy for hours.

FINISHED SIZE About 16" (42 cm) face circumference, 14" (35.5 cm) face length, and 14" (35.5 cm) long from top of head to base of neck, after felting and stuffing; sock measures about 13½" (34.5 cm) foot circumference, 15" (38 cm) leg length from cuff to bottom of foot, and 14½" (37 cm) foot length from back of heel to tip of toe, before felting.

YARN Worsted weight (#4 Medium).
Shown here: Brown Sheep Lamb's Pride Worsted (85% wool; 15% mohair; 190 yd [173 m]/4 oz): #M51 winter blue (MC), 2 skeins; #M115 oatmeal (tan) and #M175 bronze patina (brown), 1 skein each.

NEEDLES Size U.S. 8 (5 mm): set of 4 or 5 double-pointed (dpn). Exact gauge is not important.

NOTIONS Marker (m), tapestry needle; about 1 yd (1 meter) smooth cotton yarn; 3 tennis balls to facilitate felting; size H/8 (5 mm) crochet hook; four ¾" (2 cm) metal D-rings; two 1" (2.5 cm) buttons for eyes; polyester fiber stuffing

GAUGE About 20 stitches and 28 rows = 4" (10 cm) in stockinette stitch, worked in rounds, before felting.

LEG (Neck)

With MC, CO 72 sts. Arrange sts evenly on three dpn, place marker (pm), and join for working in rnds. Work k2, p2 rib for 4 rnds.

Eyelet rnd *Yo, k2, yo, p2; rep from *.

Next rnd *K2tog, ssk, p2; rep from *.

Cont in established rib until piece measures 5" (12.5 cm) from CO. Change to St st and knit 4 rnds. With tan, knit 2 rnds. With MC, knit 4 rnds. With tan, knit 1 rnd, then purl 2 rnds, then knit 1 rnd. With MC, knit 4 rnds. With brown, knit 1 rnd, purl 3 rnds, knit 1 rnd. With MC, work even until piece measures 9" (23 cm) from CO, ending 18 sts before end-of-rnd m.

HEEL (Head)

Work 36 sts back and forth in rows as foll:

Heel Flap

Row 1 (WS) Sl 1, p35.

Row 2 (RS) Sl 1, k35.

Rep Rows 1 and 2 for a total of 36 rows ending with WS Row 1—18 chain edge sts at each selvedge edge.

Turn Heel

Work short-rows as foll:

Row 1 (RS) Sl 1, k19, ssk, k1, turn work.

Row 2 Sl 1, p5, p2tog, p1, turn work.

Row 3 Sl 1, knit to 1 st before gap formed on previous row, ssk (1 st each side of gap), k1, turn work.

Row 4 Sl 1, purl to 1 st before gap formed on previous row, p2tog (1 st each side of gap), p1, turn work.

Rep Rows 3 and 4 until all heel sts have been worked, ending with a WS row and omitting the final k1 on the last rep of Row 3 and omitting the final p1 on the last rep of Row 4—20 sts rem.

Gussets

Rejoin for working in rnds as foll:

Rnd 1 With Needle 1, k20 heel sts, then pick up and knit 18 sts along selvedge edge of heel flap; with Needle 2, k36 held instep sts; with Needle 3, pick up and knit 18 sts along other selvedge edge of heel flap, then knit the first 10 heel sts again—92 sts total.

Rnd 2 On Needle 1, knit to last 2 sts, ssk; on Needle 2, knit; on Needle 3, ssk, knit to end—2 sts dec'd.

Rnd 3 Knit.

Rep Rnds 2 and 3 until 72 sts rem. Knit 1 rnd.

FOOT (Face)

Change to tan and work basketweave patt as foll:

Rnds 1–4 *K2, p2; rep from *.

Rnds 5–8 *P2, k2; rep from *.

Rep Rnds 1–8 once more, then work Rnds 1–4 once again—20 rnds total.

Change to MC and work even in St st for 6 rnds.

TOE (Nose)

Change to brown. Knit 1 rnd.

Dec Rnd 1 *K7, k2tog; rep from *—64 sts rem.

Knit 3 rnds.

Dec Rnd 2 *K6, k2tog; rep from *—56 sts rem.
Knit 3 rnds.
Dec Rnd 3 *K5, k2tog; rep from *—48 sts rem.
Knit 3 rnds.
Dec Rnd 4 *K4, k2tog; rep from *—40 sts rem.
Knit 3 rnds.
Dec Rnd 5 *K3, k2tog; rep from *—32 sts rem.
Knit 1 rnd.
Dec Rnd 6 *K2, k2tog; rep from *—24 sts rem.
Knit 1 rnd.
Dec Rnd 7 *K1, k2tog; rep from *—16 sts rem.
Knit 1 rnd.
Dec Rnd 8 *K2tog; rep from *—8 sts rem.
Cut yarn, leaving an 8" (20.5 cm) tail. Thread tail on a
tapestry needle. Pull needle through rem sts 2 times, pull
tight to close hole, and fasten off on WS.

OUTER EAR (make 2)

With brown, CO 23 sts. Knitting the first and last st of
every row to facilitate seaming later, work the center 21 sts
in St st (knit on RS; purl on WS) for 5 rows.
Dec row (RS) K1 (edge st), ssk, knit to last 3 sts, k2tog, k1
    (edge st)—2 sts dec'd.
Work 3 rows even. Rep the last 4 rows 6 more times—9 sts
rem. [Rep dec row, then work 1 row even] 2 times—5 sts rem.
Next row (RS) K1, sl 2 sts kwise, k1, p2sso, k1—3 sts rem.
P3tog—1 st rem. Cut yarn and pull tail through rem loop
to secure.

INNER EAR (make 2)

With tan, CO 21 sts. Work in seed st as foll:
Next row (WS) *K1, p1; rep from * to last st, k1.
Next row (RS) *K1, p1; rep from * to last st, k1.

BRIDLE

Thread the bridle cord through the D-rings on
the neck and face, beginning at point 1 and
ending at point 9. Even out the ends, secure at
each side of the neck tie, then tie together in
an overhand knot.

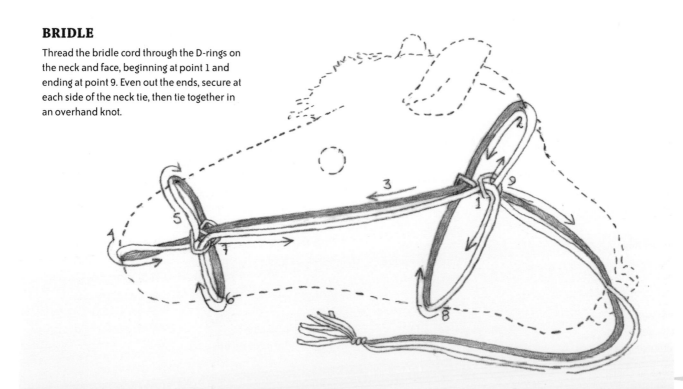

Cont alternating knits and purls every st and every row for 3 more rows—5 rows total. Keeping in patt as established, dec 1 st each end of needle (work either k2tog or p2tog on first 2 and last 2 sts as necessary to maintain patt) every 4th row 8 times—5 sts rem. Work 1 WS row even. Rep dec row—3 sts rem.

Next row K3tog—1 st rem. Cut yarn and pull tail through rem loop to secure.

With brown threaded on a tapestry needle and WS facing tog, sew inner ears to outer ears. Sew ears to heel of sock, positioned along short-row decs on each side of heel cap shaping.

FINISHING

Weave in loose ends.

Felting

Thread smooth cotton yarn through eyelets on leg ribbing to prevent eyelets from felting tog. Place head, three tennis balls (to increase agitation), and a small amount of detergent in washing machine set for lowest water level and warm water. Run through the regular wash cycle until the desired amount of felting has occurred (20 minutes for piece shown). Run through rinse and spin cycles. Pull to shape and lay flat to dry.

Neck Tie

With MC and crochet hook, make a chain (see Glossary) about 18" (45.5 cm) long. Fasten off. Beg and end at the center front, thread tie in and out of eyelets as you remove cotton waste yarn.

Stuffing

Stuff sock with polyester fiberfill until uniformly dense. Pull tie tightly to secure filling and tie into a bow.

Mane

Cut a piece of cardboard 6½" (16.5 cm) wide and 9" (23 cm) long. Wrap brown yarn around short width

64 times. Cut along each short end to make 128 lengths. Attach the fringe bet the ears as foll: Hold 2 lengths tog, fold them in half, then use a crochet hook to pull the fold through a stitch on the felted body. Pull the loose ends through the fold to secure.

Bridle

With tan and dpn, CO 4 sts. Work 4-st I-cord (see Glossary) until piece measures about 3½" yd (3.2 meters) from CO.

Next row Sl 2, k2tog, p2sso—1 st rem.

Cut yarn and thread tail through rem st to fasten off.

With matching thread and sharp-point sewing needle, sew one D-ring to each side at the base of the heel flap and one D-ring to each side of the nose at the color change, aligned with the previous rings. Thread the cord through the rings and around the head as shown on page 31. Sew the buttons to the face, each about 3" (7 cm) below an ear. Place head on top of broomstick or pole.

LEARN-TO DISHRAG

You have to try a handknitted dish-rag to appreciate its qualities. For Therese Inverso, a dishrag is a gift for the knitter as well as the recipi-ent. Use it as a sampler to learn a new cast-on, bind-off, or a differ-ent way to knit. If you normally tension the yarn in your right hand in the English "throwing" method, learn how to tension the yarn in your left hand in the Continental "picking" method, or vice versa. Tension problems, holes, and mis-shaped stitches won't interfere with its ability to wipe counters!

Using the method of your choice, CO 35 sts. Knit 8 rows for a border.
Set-up row (RS) K5, place marker (pm), knit and purl the center 25 sts randomly, pm, k5.

Cont as established until piece measures about 7½" (19 cm). Knit 8 rows. Using the method of your choice, loosely BO all sts. Weave in loose ends.

FINISHED SIZE About 8½" (21.5 cm) wide and 8½" (21.5 cm) long.

YARN Worsted weight (#4 Medium).
Shown here: Lily Sugar 'n Cream (100% cotton/4 oz). One ball will make several dish-rags. Shown in #18003 cream and # 18083 cornflower.

NEEDLES Size U.S. 7 (4 mm).

NOTIONS Markers (m); tapestry needle.

GAUGE About 16 stitches and 30 rows = 4" (10 cm) in garter stitch. Exact gauge is not critical but the stitches should be loose enough that the dishrag will air-dry overnight.

transitions
HAT & SCARF

For this simple cabled hat-and-scarf set, **Ruthie Nussbaum** kept things interesting by working in gradational color stripes. She knitted with three strands of yarn throughout, but changed one strand at a time to create smooth gradations from dark to light (and back to dark for the scarf). The eight-stitch pattern repeat is easily memorized and the knitting goes quickly at a gauge of 4½ stitches to the inch.

FINISHED SIZE *Hat:* 19" (48.5 cm) circumference and 7½" (19 cm) tall, after blocking. To fit an adult. *Scarf:* About 4¼" (11 cm) wide and 72" (183 cm) long, after blocking.

YARN Fingering weight (#1 Super Fine).
Shown here: Dale of Norway Baby Ull (100% wool; 180 yd [164 m]/50 g):

#4227 (burgundy; dark), #4018 (red; medium), #3718 (tomato red; light) 3 skeins each for both scarf and hat.

NEEDLES Size U.S. 9 (5.5 mm): straight or circular (cir) for scarf; 16" (40 cm) cir and set of 4 or 5 double-pointed (dpn) for hat. Adjust needle size if necessary to obtain the correct gauge.

NOTIONS Cable needle (cn); tapestry needle; marker (m) for hat only.

GAUGE 18 stitches and 25 rows = 4" (10 cm) in stockinette stitch with three strands of yarn.

stitch guide

+ HAT PATTERN (multiple of 7 sts)

Rnds 1, 5, and 7 *K4, p3; rep from * to end of rnd.

Rnds 2, 4, and 6 *K4, p1, yo, p2tog; rep from * to end of rnd.

Rnd 3 *Sl 2 sts onto cn and hold in back, k2, k2 from cn, p3; rep from * to end of rnd.

Rnd 8 Rep Rnd 2.

Repeat Rounds 1–8 for pattern.

+ SCARF PATTERN (multiple of 7 sts + 5)

Rows 1, 5, and 7 (RS) K1, p3, *k4, p3; rep from * to last st, k1.

Rows 2, 4, and 6 K2, yo, k2tog, *p4, k1, yo, k2tog; rep from * to last st, k1.

Row 3 K1, p3, *sl 2 sts onto cn and hold in back, k2, k2 from cn, p3; rep from * to last st, k1.

Row 8 Rep Row 2.

Repeat Rows 1–8 for pattern.

HAT

With three strands of the dark shade held tog and cir needle, CO 84 sts. Place marker (pm) and join for working in rnds, being careful not to twist sts. Rep Rnd 1 of hat patt (see Stitch Guide) 4 times for border—4 rnds total. Work Rnds 2–8 of patt, then rep Rnds 1–8 three more times, then work Rnds 1–3 once more and *at the same time* change colors as foll: Work with three strands dark for 2½" (6.5 cm), work with two strands dark and one strand medium for ½" (1.3 cm), work with one strand dark and two strands medium for ½" (1.3 cm), work with three strands medium for 1½" (3.8 cm), work with two strands medium and one strand light for ½" (1.3 cm), work with one strand medium and two strands light for ½" (1.3 cm)—piece measures about 6" (15 cm) from CO.

Shape Top

Work with three strands of light to end, dec as foll, changing to dpn when there are too few sts to fit comfortably around cir needle:

Rnd 1 K4, p2tog, *p1, k4, p2tog; rep from * to last st, p1—72 sts rem.

Rnds 2, 4, and 6 Knit.

Rnd 3 *K4, p2tog; rep from * to end of rnd—60 sts rem.

Rnd 5 *K3, p2tog; rep from * to end of rnd—48 sts rem.

Rnd 7 *K2, p2tog; rep from * across round—36 sts rem.

Rnd 8 *K1, p2tog; rep from * to end of rnd—24 sts rem.

Rnd 9 *K2tog; rep from * to end of rnd—12 sts rem.

Rnd 10 *K2tog; rep from * to end of rnd—6 sts rem.

Cut yarn, leaving an 8" (20.5 cm) tail. Thread tail on tapestry needle and run through rem sts 2 times, pull tight to gather sts, and fasten off to WS of hat.

Weave in loose ends. Block lightly.

SCARF

With three strands of the dark shade held tog, CO 26 sts. Work in scarf patt (see Stitch Guide) and *at the same time* change colors as foll: Work with three strands dark yarn for 8" (20.5 cm), work with two strands dark and one strand medium for 3" (7.5 cm), work with one strand dark and two strands medium for 4" (10 cm), work with three strands medium for 6" (15 cm), work with two strands medium and one strand light for 2" (5 cm), work with one strand medium and two strands light for 4" (10 cm), work with three strands light for 10" (25.5 cm), work with two strands light and one strand medium for 4" (10 cm), work with one strand light and two strands medium for 2" (5 cm), work with three strands medium for 6" (15 cm), work with two strands medium and one strand dark for 4" (10 cm), work with one strand medium and two strands dark for 3" (7.5 cm), work with three strands dark for 8" (20.5 cm), ending with Row 4 of patt. BO all sts.

Weave in loose ends. Block lightly to finished measurements.

felted
OVEN MITTS

*T*herese Inverso has sewn oven mitts out of felted thrift-shop sweaters for years. For knitters, she's developed a knitted version that has the same attractive feature—extra thickness across the palm and the front of the thumb to give substantial protection when lifting hot pans out of the oven. Begin with an oversized mitten knitted with single-ply unspun Icelandic wool at a gauge of five stitches to the inch, then felt it into a thick and sturdy mitt. A quick haircut with small scissors eliminated any stray fibers on the surface.

FINISHED SIZE About 20¼" (51.5 cm) hand circumference and 17½" (44.5 cm) total length, before felting; about 11" (28 cm) hand circumference and 9½" (24 cm) total length, after felting.

YARN Worsted weight (#4 Medium). *Shown here:* School-house Press Unspun Icelandic Wool (100% Icelandic wool; 300 yd [274 m]/3½ oz): eggplant (MC) and gold (CC), 1 wheel each. There will be enough yarn to make a second mitt in the opposite colorway. Unfelted mitt shown on page 41 worked in sumac (burgundy) (MC) and gold (CC).

NEEDLES *Mitts:* size U.S. 6 (4 mm): 16" (40 cm) circular (cir) and two 24" (60 cm) cir. *I-cord trim:* size 7 (4.5 mm): set of 3 double-pointed (dpn). Adjust needle size if necessary to obtain the correct gauge.

NOTIONS Coil-less safety pin; tapestry needle; size H/8 (5 mm) crochet hook; about 7 yd (6.4 m) total of smooth cotton waste yarn; short trimming scissors; toothbrush.

GAUGE 20 stitches and 24 rounds = 4" (10 cm) In stockinette stitch on smaller needles, worked in rounds, before felting.

NOTES
+ Unspun Icelandic wool requires gentle knitting. Take your time when knitting and enjoy the process. If the wool breaks, repair by wet splicing (see page 44).

+ The color pattern is worked in the round following Joyce Williams's method of using two 24" (60 cm) circular needles—the palm stitches on one needle and the back-of-hand stitches on the other needle. When knitting, use both ends of the same needle to work the palm stitches and both ends of the other needle to work the back-of-hand stitches.

MITT

With shorter cir needle, smooth cotton string, and using the crocheted-on method (see Glossary), provisionally CO 88 sts. Leaving a 6" (15 cm) tail, knit the sts with MC, then join for working in rnds, being careful not to twist sts. Knit 1 rnd. Place a coil-less safety pin in the last rnd to mark beg of rnd. Move this pin up as the knitting grows.

Cuff and Lower Hand

Rnd 1 *K2, p2; rep from *.
Rnd 2 Knit.
Rep these 2 rnds 5 more times—12 rnds total. Knit every rnd until piece measures 8½" (21.5 cm) from CO.

Mark Thumb Opening

K12, knit the next 20 sts with 1 yard (1 meter) of cotton waste yarn, sl these 20 sts back onto left needle and knit them again with working yarn, knit to end of rnd.

Upper Hand

Cont even until piece measures 1½" (3.8 cm) from marked thumb opening. Rearrange sts on two 24" (60 cm) cir needles so that there are 44 palm sts on one cir needle with the 20 thumb sts bordered by 12 sts on each side and so that there are 44 back-of-hand sts on the other cir needle. The palm sts will be knitted in the checkered patt; the back-of-hand sts will be knitted in stripes. Turn the work inside out so that the purl side of the fabric faces outward and the knit side faces inward (pull the wheel of yarn through the knitted tube). For the remainder of the mitt, knit on the "far side" of the tube as illustrated at right. Join CC. Stranding the unused color loosely, work Row 1 of Check chart across 44 palm sts, loosely twist MC and CC around each other, then knit Row 1 of Stripe chart across 44 back-of-hand sts, being careful to pull the yarn firmly bet needles so there are no loose sts.
Next rnd (Rnd 2 of charts) Bring the MC strand across the WS of the palm to the beg of the rnd, allowing it to

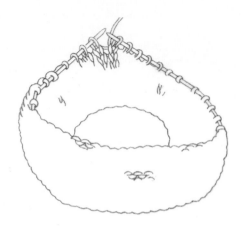

KNITTING ON THE FAR SIDE

To help ensure that the stranded yarn is kept loose, use Joyce Williams's method of "knitting on the far side." Turn the work inside out so that the wrong side faces outward and the right side (public side) faces inside.

hang loosely (about 14" [35.5 cm]), and twist the two colors around each other, work Rnd 2 of Check chart across 44 palm sts, using your needle tip to catch the loose strand between every second and third st as you go, then work Rnd 2 of Stripe chart across 44 back-of-hand sts.
Cont in this manner through Rnd 12 of charts, then rep Rnds 1–12 once more.

Shape Top

(Rnd 1 of patts) *Keeping in patt, k1, ssk, work to last 3 palm sts, k2tog, k1; rep from * across back-of-hand sts—4 sts dec'd; 42 sts rem each for palm and back of hand. Work 1 rnd even in patt. Rep the shaping of the last 2 rnds 5 more times, ending with Rnd 12 of charts—64 sts rem; 32 sts each for palm and back of hand. Cut off CC, leaving a 12" (30.5 cm) tail. Cut off MC, leaving a 2½ yard (2.25 meter) tail.

Before felting, the mitt is gigantic!

□ main color—knit on RS

■ contrast color—knit on RS

◻ ssk on RS, in MC or CC

◻ k2tog, in MC or CC

□ pattern repeat

● marker

Check

11
9
7
5
3
1

work 8 sts bet markers
5 times - 40 sts

Stripe

11
9
7
5
3
1

work 8 sts bet markers
5 times - 40 sts

Thumb Back

15
13
11
9
7
5
3
1

Thumb Front

15
13
11
9
7
5
3
1

Thread the MC tail on a tapestry needle so that the yarn is doubled and a 12" (30.5 cm) tail hangs inside the mitt. Twist the tapestry needle gently so that the two strands twist around each other to strengthen the yarn. Turn the piece RS out. Using the Kitchener st (see Glossary), graft the rem sts tog. Work the tails into the stranded yarn on the WS of the palm or along the boundaries between the palm and back-of-hand sts.

Thumb

Carefully remove cotton waste yarn at thumb, placing the 20 bottom sts on one 24" (60 cm) cir needle (for the back of the thumb) and the top 19 sts on the other 24" (60 cm) cir needle (for the palm side of the thumb), making sure that the sts are in the proper orientation on the needles. Work in rnds as foll:

Rnd 1 Leaving an 8" (20.5 cm) tail, join MC and k20 back sts, then pick up and knit 2 sts in the gap bet the 2 needles; with the palm needle, pick up and knit 1 st in the gap, k19 palm sts, then pick up and knit 2 sts in the other gap—44 sts total; 22 sts on each needle.

Rnd 2 *Ssk, k18, k2tog; rep from * once—40 sts rem.

Rnds 3, 4, and 5 Knit.

Rnd 6 (dec rnd) *K1, ssk, knit to last 3 sts on needle, k2tog, k1; rep from * once—36 sts rem.

Rnds 7, 8, and 9 Knit.

Next rnd K18 back sts, turn work inside out (gently squeeze the yarn ball through the opening) for working on the "far side" as for the upper hand.

Work Rnds 1–15 of Thumb charts and *at the same time* dec 4 sts as before on Rnds 4, 7, 10, and 13 of chart—20 sts rem. Work even through Rnd 15. Cut off CC, leaving a 12" (30.5 cm) tail. Beg where MC is already attached, knit 1 rnd with MC. Cut off MC, leaving a 36" (91.5 cm) tail.

Thread the MC tail on a tapestry needle so that the yarn is doubled and an 8" (20.5 cm) tail hangs inside the thumb. Turn the piece right side out. Twist two strands around

each other, then use the Kitchener st to graft the rem sts tog. Work the tails into the stranded yarn on the WS of the thumb. Tighten the loose sts at the base of the thumb with other tails.

Cut three lengths of wool, each 24" (61 cm) long. Turn thumb inside out. Thread one strand on tapestry needle and pull it halfway through the strands at the center of the top of the thumb so that that there are two 12" (30.5 cm) tails. Weave each tail in and out of the strands on the palm side of the thumb to thicken the thumb area and make it more insulating. Work the other two lengths on each side of the first.

FINISHING
I-Cord Edging

Carefully remove waste yarn from crochet CO, placing the live sts in their correct orientation on 16" (40 cm) cir needle—88 sts. With waste yarn and using the crochet method, provisionally CO 3 sts onto 1 dpn. Transfer these 3 sts onto left tip of cir needle. With CC and a second dpn, work Joyce Williams's method for contrasting attached I-cord as foll: *K2, sl 1, yo, k1 (live st from CO), pass the slipped st and the yo over the k1 st—3 sts on left dpn. Transfer these 3 sts onto left tip of cir needle. Rep from * until 3 sts rem. To finish, remove waste yarn from provisional 3-st CO and place these 3 sts onto an empty dpn—3 sts each on 2 needles. Hold the needles parallel with the WS of the I-cord edging facing tog and RS facing outward. Using a third needle, *k2tog (1 st from each needle); rep from *—3 sts rem.

BBQ MITTS

It's easy to make a longer mitt for grilling. All you need is an extra wheel of MC. Knit the lower hand to 17" (43 cm) before marking the thumb. During felting, stretch out the lower hand and cuff to ensure that it is wide enough.

I-Cord Loop

Work 3-st I-cord (see Glossary) for 8" (20.5 cm). Cut yarn, leaving an 8" (20.5 cm) tail. Thread tail on a tapestry needle and sew live sts securely to base of cord, forming a loop. To reinforce cord, cut a 20" (51 cm) strand of CC and thread it on a tapestry needle. Pull the yarn through to the halfway point so there is 10" (25.5 cm) of yarn on each side of needle and work with the yarn doubled. Thread the double strand through the center of the I-cord sts two times, then secure the ends into the base of the edging.

Felting

Fill the washing machine with enough hot water to completely cover the mitts and allow enough room for them to slosh around. Add about half the amount of laundry detergent you would normally use for a load of a similar size and about an eighth of a cup of baking soda to ensure an alkaline solution. Turn the mitt(s) inside out and place in washer. Run the washer through the entire wash cycle. Stop the machine after the water has drained and remove all the wool lint sticking to the mitt(s) and sides of machine (save this lint to make felt balls—see page 45).

Allow the washer to proceed through the rinse and spin cycles. Remove lint. Rep the cycle, using about half as much detergent as before and the same amount of baking soda, removing lint between cycles and pulling the knitting to make sure that the two sides of the thumb or hand do not felt tog. Turn the mitt(s) right side out for the remainder of the felting process. Rep the process until the mitt(s) measures about 5" (12.5 cm) wide and 9" (23 cm) long (the mitts shown went through four complete cycles).

Place the wet mitt(s) in the dryer on the delicate setting for about 10 minutes to remove additional lint (save this lint, too). Gently tug the damp mitt(s) into shape and lay flat to dry.

Trim Surface

Trim the "hairs" on the outer surface of the mitts with a pair of 5" (12.5 cm) scissors. Use a toothbrush to clear away the cut hairs. Trim the lower 1" (2.5 cm) of the inside in the same manner (save the trimmings).

Place a pressing cloth on top of the mitt and with the iron at the cotton setting, steam-press the mitt for a final finish.

WET-SPLICE WOOL YARNS

To splice together two balls of wool yarn, untwist an inch or two from the end of each ball (**Figure 1**), overlap the raveled ends (**Figure 2**), and moisten them with saliva. Place the wet overlapped loose fibers in one palm and use your other palm to vigorously rub the two ends together (**Figure 3**). The moisture and friction will cause the two yarn ends to felt together. This trick may not work with superwash wool yarn.

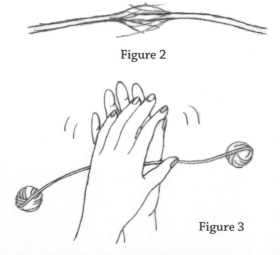

Figure 2

Figure 1

Figure 3

WOOL LINT JUGGLING BALLS

If you can make meatballs or snowballs, you can make a set of designer juggling balls. Simply gather the lint produced from felting other projects in the washing machine and shape it into a ball (with a little elbow grease, of course).

Mix about 10 parts water to 1 part dishwashing liquid and place this solution in a squirt bottle. Working over a dishpan, to catch any wayward lint, gently tease apart a handful of wool lint. Roll the lint into a ball between your palms, sprinkle it with soap solution, and compress the lint together as you continue to roll it in your hands. Cont to add layers of lint, dousing it with the soap solution, and roll it between your palms until the ball is about the size of a girl's softball. If desired, wrap some single-ply wool around the ball for decoration. Continue to roll and compress the ball until it is as dense as possible (this will take a bit of "elbow grease") to complete the soft stage of felting.

Place the ball in the leg of a nylon stocking (if you're making several balls, put each in a separate stocking leg or tie knots in the stocking between balls in the same leg). Place the stocking and balls into a lingerie bag and put it in the washing machine with every load of laundry (avoid loads that contain bleach). After many washings, the ball will be quite hard (and quite a bit smaller). Allow the ball to dry thoroughly (use the dryer, if desired).

FINISHED SIZE About 7½" (19 cm) in circumference, after felting. Actual size will depend on felting.

YARN Wool felt retrieved during the felting of other projects, wool fleece, or bits of unspun wool.

NOTIONS Small amount of dishwashing liquid; squirt bottle; nylon stocking; lingerie bag; single-ply wool for decoration (optional).

gentleman's
SCARF

*V*éronik **Avery** designed this manly scarf out of a
sumptuous cashmere-silk-blend yarn knitted at a
fine gauge. Your fingers will never tire of the feel of the
yarn and the simple cables and embossed stitch pattern
will hold your interest through every tiny stitch. To make
the two sides identical, Véronik worked the scarf in two
halves, each beginning with a decorative Channel Island
cast-on, which are grafted together at the other ends.

FINISHED SIZE About 8"
(20.5 cm) wide and 40½" (103 cm)
long.

YARN Sportweight (#2 Fine).
Shown here: Trendsetter Bollicina
(65% cashmere, 35% silk; 145 yd
[133 m]/50 g): #248 gold, 4 balls.

NEEDLES Size U.S. 2 (2.75 mm).
Adjust needle size if necessary to
obtain the correct gauge.

NOTIONS Stitch holders; tapestry
needle.

GAUGE 40 stitches and 52 rows
= 4" (10 cm) in charted pattern.

☐ knit on RS; purl on WS

• purl on RS; knit on WS

⟋⟍ 2/2 RC: sl 2 sts onto cable needle and hold in back, k2, k2 from cable needle

⟍⟋ 2/2 LC: sl 2 sts onto cable needle and hold in front, k2, k2 from cable needle

☐ pattern repeat

Cables & Zigzags

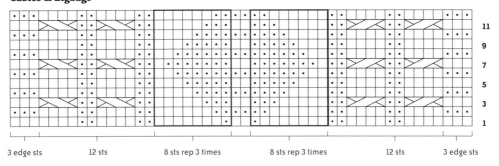

3 edge sts   12 sts   8 sts rep 3 times   8 sts rep 3 times   12 sts   3 edge sts

11
9
7
5
3
1

SCARF

First Half

Using the Channel Island method (see below), CO 80 sts. Knit 8 rows. Work Rows 1–12 of Cables & Zigzags chart until piece measures about 20" (51 cm) from CO, ending with Row 1 of chart. Place sts on holder. Cut yarn, leaving a 12" (30.5 cm) tail.

Second Half

CO and work as for first half, ending on Row 11 of chart (instead of Row 1). Cut yarn, leaving a 24" (61 cm) tail.

FINISHING

Block pieces lightly. With yarn from second half threaded on a tapestry needle, use the Kitchener st (see Glossary) to graft the live sts of each half tog (or BO the sts for each of the two halves and sew them tog). Weave in loose ends. Block to finished measurements.

CHANNEL-ISLAND CAST-ON

This cast-on requires three strands of yarn. Use both ends from a center-pull ball (the inner and outer tails) for the double strand and the working end from a second ball for the single strand. Hold the three strands together and make a slipknot, leaving a 4" (10 cm) tail. Place the slipknot on the right needle. The slipknot counts as the first stitch. Wrap the double strands counterclockwise around your thumb two times. Place the remaining single strand over your left finger. The double strands will form the beaded stitches and the single strand will form the regular stitches. *Make a yarnover on the needle with the single strand (Figure 1). Hold the yarnover in place on the needle as you insert the needle up through all the loops on your thumb, grab the single strand, and bring it back through the thumb loops (Figure 2). Drop the thumb loops and tighten all three yarns to form two more stitches. Repeat from * for the desired number of stitches. Cut the double strands, leaving 4" (10 cm) tails to weave in later and continue to work with the single yarn. *Note:* Because the slipknot counts as a stitch, there will be an odd number of stitches. To create an even number of stitches, work two stitches into the slipknot on the first row of knitting.

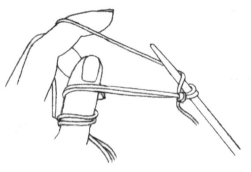

Figure 1

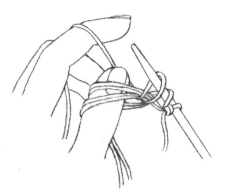

Figure 2

fresco
LEG WARMERS

*H*andknitted socks are usually hidden under shoes and pants, but leg warmers are always on display, and they let you wear skirts in winter without suffering cold legs. In this pair, **Pam Allen** worked a soft wool-alpaca-blend yarn in a simple-to-follow feminine lace pattern. She designed them to have a snug fit that will show off your legs to their best advantage—no bulky wrinkles allowed! Each leg is worked in the round from the cuff to the top, with increases incorporated into a rib pattern along the way to taper the upper leg.

FINISHED SIZE About 7 (8½, 10)" (18 [21.5, 25.5] cm) circumference at ankle and about 8 (10, 11½)" (20.5 [25.5, 29] cm) circumference at upper leg, unstretched. Leg warmers shown measure 7" (18 cm) circumference at ankle.

YARN Sportweight (#2 Fine). *Shown here:* Classic Elite Fresco (60% wool, 30% baby alpaca, 10% angora; 164 yd [150 m]/50 g): #5320 Ashley blue, 4 (4, 5) skeins.

NEEDLES Size U.S. 3 (3.25 mm): set of 4 or 5 double-pointed (dpn). Adjust needle size if necessary to obtain the correct gauge.

NOTIONS Markers (m); tapestry needle.

GAUGE 42 stitches and 44 rounds = 4" (10 cm) in lace pattern, worked in rounds.

Lower Leg

☐	knit on RS
•	purl on RS
M	make-1 (see Glossary)
O	yarnover
λ	sl 1 kwise, k2tog, psso
▨	no stitch—Ignore gray square(s) and work next non-gray square
☐	pattern repeat
↓	marker

Work 15 sts between markers
4 (5, 6) times—60 (75, 90) sts.

LEGWARMER (make 2)

CO 74 (90, 104) sts. Arrange the sts evenly among 3 or 4 dpn, place marker (pm), and join for working in rnds, being careful not to twist sts. Work in k1, p1 rib until piece measures 1¼" (3.2 cm) from CO, inc 1 (0, 1) st on last rnd—75 (90, 105) sts. Work Rnds 1–9 of Lower Leg chart.

Inc rnd: (Rnd 10) Work next 60 (75, 90) sts as charted, k2, M1 (see Glossary), work next 13 sts as charted, M1—2 sts inc'd.

Knitting the inc'd sts, work 9 rnds in patt as established, then rep inc rnd 4 more times, ending with Rnd 50 and working the inc'd sts into k2, p2 rib when there are sufficient sts to do so—85 (100, 115) sts. Work Rnds 51–100 of Upper Leg chart, working incs on Rnds 60, 70, and 80 as indicated on chart—91 (106, 121) sts; piece measures about 20½" (52 cm) from CO after Rnd 100 is completed.

Upper Leg

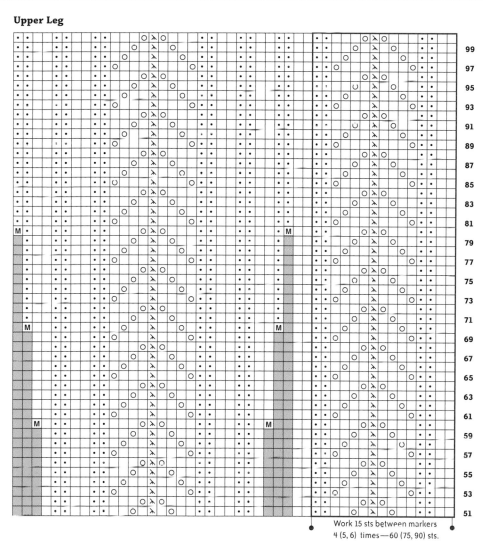

99
97
95
93
91
89
87
85
83
81
79
77
75
73
71
69
67
65
63
61
59
57
55
53
51

Work 15 sts between markers
4 (5, 6) times—60 (75, 90) sts.

Next rnd Dec 1 (0, 1) st, work in rib to end—90 (106, 120)
sts rem.
Work even in k1, p1 rib for 1¼" (3.2 cm). Loosely BO all sts
in patt.

FINISHING
Weave in loose ends. Block.

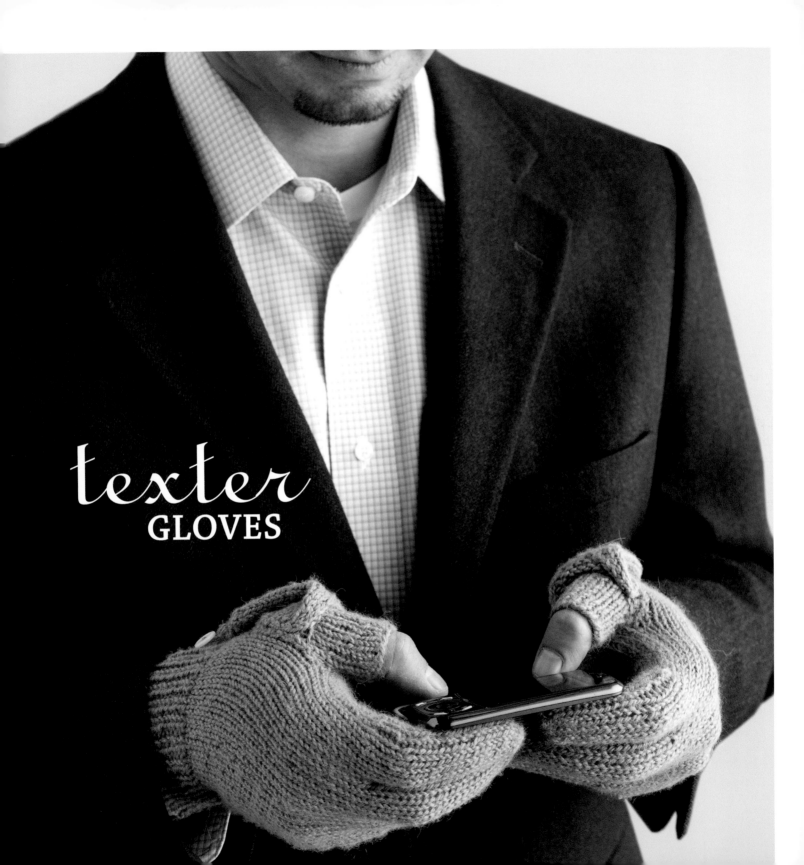

texter GLOVES

For those who just love to communicate via text message, even in frigid temperatures, **Kim Hamlin** designed a pair of gloves that will help stave off frostbite. Remove the thumb flaps for controlled texting while your other fingers stay warm. The fingers (and thumb) are worked from the top down for a just-right fit, then added to the hand as it is worked from the base of the fingers to the cuff. The soft alpaca yarn ensures comfort even for non-texters.

FINISHED SIZE About 7 (8½, 9¾)" (18 [21.5, 23] cm) hand circumference and 7½ (8, 8¾)" (19 [20.5, 22] cm) hand length from base of palm to tip of middle finger. Gloves shown measure 8½" (21.5 cm) hand circumference.

YARN Sportweight (#2 Fine). *Shown here:* Blue Sky Alpacas Alpaca Sport (100% alpaca; 110 yd [100 m]/50 g): avocado, 3 (3, 4) skeins.

NEEDLES *Hand:* size U.S. 5 (3.75 mm): set of 5 double-pointed (dpn). *Cuff:* size U.S. 3 (3.25 mm): set of 5 dpn. Adjust needle size if necessary to obtain the correct gauge.

NOTIONS Size D/3 (3.25 mm) crochet hook; markers (m); tapestry needle; two ⅜" (1 cm) buttons.

GAUGE 11 stitches and 16 rounds = 2" (5 cm) in stockinette stitch on larger needles, worked in rounds.

FINGERS
Index Finger

Work crochet-loop CO as foll: make a slipknot and place on crochet hook (see Glossary for crochet instructions). Ch 2—1 loop on hook. *Insert hook into first ch, wrap yarn and pull through first loop. Wrap yarn around hook and pull through the new loop just created (this loop remains on crochet hook). Rep from * 4 (5, 6) more times—5 (6, 7) loops on hook. Place all loops onto a single larger dpn. Slide sts to other tip of dpn and bring yarn across back as for working I-cord (see Glossary) as foll: [K1f&b (see Glossary)] 4 (5, 6) times, k1—9 (11, 13) sts. Cont as 9 (11, 13)-st I-cord (there will be a loose ladder across the back of the sts) until piece measures 2½ (2¾, 3)" (6.5 [7, 7.5] cm) or desired length. Cut yarn, leaving a 4" (10 cm) tail. Transform the loose ladder along the back of the I-cord into another st as foll: Insert crochet hook into center hole at tip of finger and pull the first horizontal bar of the ladder through—1 st on hook. *Grab the next horizontal bar with the hook and pull this bar through the st on the hook; rep from * until all horizontal bars have been worked. Pull the yarn tail through the loop on the hook to form a new st, then transfer this st to the front of the needle—10 (12, 14) sts total. Place all sts onto an empty smaller dpn. Set aside.

Middle Finger

Work as for index finger until piece measures 2¾ (3, 3¼)" (7 [7.5, 8.5] cm) or desired length. Transform the loose ladder into another st as for index finger—10 (12, 14) sts total. Place all sts onto a second empty smaller dpn. Set aside.

Ring Finger

Work as for index finger. Place sts onto a third empty smaller dpn. Set aside.

Little Finger

Work crochet-loop CO as for index finger until there are 4 (5, 6) sts. Transfer sts onto a single larger dpn. Slide sts to other tip of dpn and bring yarn across back as for working I-cord as foll: [K1f&b] 3 (4, 5) times, k1—7 (9, 11) sts. Cont as I-cord until piece measures 2 (2¼, 2½)" (5 [5.5, 6.5] cm) or desired length. Transform the loose ladder into another st as for other fingers—8 (10, 12) sts total. Place sts onto a fourth empty smaller dpn. Set aside.

Thumb

With larger dpn, CO 9 (11, 13) sts. Work as I-cord until piece measures about 1¼ (1¼, 1½)" (3.2 [3.2, 3.8] cm) or desired length from knuckle to base of thumb. Transform the loose ladder into another st, beg by twisting the top "rung" into a loop—10 (12, 14) sts total. Set aside.

JOIN FINGERS
Index, Middle, and Ring Fingers

Join index, middle, and ring fingers onto larger dpn as foll: Knit the first 5 (6, 7) index finger sts (leave rem 5 [6, 7] sts on smaller dpn as holder), knit the first 3 (3, 4) middle finger sts onto the same dpn; with a second empty larger dpn, knit the next 2 (3, 3) middle finger sts (leave rem 5 [6, 7] sts on smaller dpn as holder), then knit the first 5 (6, 7) ring finger sts; with a third empty larger dpn, knit the rem 5 (6, 7) ring finger sts, then knit the next 3 (3, 4) middle finger sts; with a fourth empty larger dpn, knit rem 2 (3, 3) middle finger sts, then knit rem 5 (6, 7) index finger sts—30 (36, 42) sts total. Place marker (pm) and join for working in rnds. Knit 4 rnds even or until piece measures about ½" (1.3 cm) from joining rnd (try on the connected fingers and add or subtract rnds as necessary to achieve a perfect fit).

Little Finger

K8 (9, 11) sts on first needle; k7 (9, 10) sts on second needle, then knit the first 4 (5, 6) little finger sts onto the same needle; knit the rem 4 (5, 6) little finger sts, then knit the 8 (9, 11) sts on the third needle; k7 (9, 10) sts on fourth needle—38 (46, 54) sts total.

UPPER HAND

Knit all rnds until piece measures about 2 (2¼, 2¾)" (5 [5.5, 7] cm) from joining rnd, or to base of thumb, ending at the boundary between the first and fourth needles.

JOIN THUMB

Knit first 5 (6, 7) thumb sts, knit to end of rnd, then knit rem 5 (6, 7) thumb sts—48 (58, 68) sts total.

Shape Thumb Gusset

Rnd 1 K6, k2tog, knit to last 8 sts, ssk, k6—2 sts dec'd; 46 (56, 66) sts rem.
Rnd 2 and all even-numbered rnds Knit.
Rnd 3 K5, k2tog, knit to last 7 sts, ssk, k5—2 sts dec'd.
Rnd 5 K4, k2tog, knit to last 6 sts, ssk, k4—2 sts dec'd.
Rnd 7 K3, k2tog, knit to last 5 sts, ssk, k3—2 sts dec'd.
Rnd 9 K2, k2tog, knit to last 4 sts, ssk, k2—2 sts dec'd.
Rnd 11 K1, k2tog, knit to last 3 sts, ssk, k1—2 sts dec'd.
Rnd 13 K2tog, knit to last 2 sts, ssk—2 sts dec'd; 34 (44, 54) sts rem.
Knit every rnd for 1" (2.5 cm) more or until piece measures to top of wrist.

CUFF

Work in k1, p1 rib for 2 (2, 2½)" (5 [5, 6.5] cm) or desired length. BO all sts in patt.

THUMB CAP

Leaving a tail at least 6" (15 cm) long, work crochet-loop CO as for index finger until there are 5 (7, 9) sts.
Next row *K1f&b; rep from *—10 (14, 18) sts.
Work as for other fingers until piece measures about 2¼ (2½, 2¾)" (5.5 [6.5, 7] cm) or to base of thumb. Use crochet hook to pick up ladder stitch and place on the left side of

dpn—11 (15, 19) sts. Turn. Purl 1 row, then knit 1 row, then purl 1 row.

Dec row (RS) Sl 1, k1, psso, knit to last 2 sts, k2tog—9 (13, 17) sts rem.

Purl 1 row. Rep the last 2 rows until 3 sts rem. Purl 1 row.

Next row (RS) Sl 1, k2tog, psso—1 st rem. Fasten off.

Button Loop

With crochet hook and tail from CO, ch 6. Work 1 row of slip st, ending at beg of ch. Fold into a loop and secure on the WS of the work.

FINISHING

With yarn threaded on a tapestry needle, sew thumb cap to glove, matching dec edges of cap to thumb gusset. Weave in loose ends, using tails to close gaps between fingers. Try on glove, fold thumb cap over thumb, and mark placement for button on cuff. Sew button in place. Block as desired.

DESIGNER *ann budd*

CANDLE COZY

Add interesting shadows to flickering candlelight by knitting lace sleeves for votive candleholders. Experiment with your own combinations of yarnovers, decreases, knit, and purl stitches to create different looks.

CO 32 sts. Arrange sts as evenly as possible on 3 or 4 dpn, place marker (pm), and join for working in rnds, being careful not to twist sts. Work Version 1 or 2 as desired.

VERSION 1

Rnd 1 Knit.

Rnd 2 Purl.

Rnd 3 *K2tog; yo; rep from *, being careful not to let yarnovers slip off ends of needles.

Rnd 4 Purl.

Rnd 5 Knit.

Rnd 6 Purl.

Rnd 7 Knit, wrapping the yarn twice around the needle with each st.

Rnd 8 Purl, dropping extra wraps.

Rep Rnds 1–8 two more times, then work Rows 1–5 once more—piece measures about 2½" (6.5 cm) from CO.

VERSION 2

Rnds 1–5 Knit.

Rnd 6 Purl.

Rnd 7 Knit, wrapping the yarn twice around the needle with each st.

Rnd 8 Purl, dropping extra wraps.

Rep Rnds 1–8 two more times, then work Rnds 1–5 once more—piece measures about 2½" (6.5 cm) from CO.

BOTH VERSIONS

Cut yarn, leaving a 28" (71 cm) tail. Thread tail on a tapestry needle and use the sewn method (see Glossary) to BO all sts. Weave in loose ends. Spray with starch, if desired.

FINISHED SIZE About 5¾" (14.5 cm) circumference and 2½" (6.5 cm) long.

YARN Laceweight (#0 Lace). *Shown here:* DMC Baroque (100% mercerized cotton; 400 yd [365 m]/75 g): about 20 yards. Shown in white.

NEEDLES Size U.S. 3 (3.25 mm): set of 4 or 5 double-pointed (dpn). Adjust needle size if necessary to obtain the correct gauge.

NOTIONS Marker (m); tapestry needle; glass candleholder measuring 6½" (16.5 cm) in circumference and 2¾" (7 cm) tall; spray starch (optional).

GAUGE 12 stitches and 16 rounds = 2" (5 cm) in stockinette stitch, worked in rounds.

motor
BABY BUNTING

Kathy Ticho designed this cozy baby bunting for the fashionable infant on the go. The bunting features a well-placed slit to accommodate a car seat strap, two-way zipper for easy diaper changes, and supersoft machine-washable yarns for easy cleaning. At a gauge of just two stitches to the inch, this colorful bunting knits up in a flash.

FINISHED SIZE About 23" (58.5 cm) wide from cuff to cuff and 23" (58.5 cm) long, excluding hood. To fit a newborn.

YARN Bulky (#6 Super Bulky). *Shown here:* Muench Yarns Big Baby (100% microfiber acrylic; 49 yd [45 m]/50 g): #5501 purple mix (MC), 7 balls. GGH Amelie (100% polyamide; 71 yd [65 m]/50 g): #20 royal blue (CC), 1 ball.

NEEDLES Size U.S. 13 (9 mm): 32" (80 cm) circular (cir) plus an extra needle for three-needle bind-off. Adjust needle size if necessary to obtain the correct gauge.

NOTIONS Markers (m); stitch holders; tapestry needle; sizes J/10 (6 mm) and M/13 (9 mm) crochet hooks; 26" (66 cm) two-way separating zipper with plastic teeth (available at www.zipperstop.com);

sharp-point sewing needle and matching thread.

GAUGE 8 stitches and 12 rows = 4" (10 cm) in stockinette stitch.

BACK

With MC and using the cable method (see Glossary), CO 14 sts. Knit 1 row. Beg with a WS row and cont in St st, use the cable method to CO 3 sts at beg of next 6 rows—32 sts. CO 1 st at beg of next 2 rows—34 sts. Work even in St st until piece measures 5½" (14 cm) from initial CO, ending with a WS row.

Shape Base and Create Slit

Note The slit is introduced at the same time as the decreases are worked; read all the way through the next section before proceeding.

Row 1 (RS) K1, ssk, knit to last 3 sts, k2tog, k1—2 sts dec'd.

Rows 2–8 Work even in St st.

Rep Rows 1–8 three more times and *at the same time* when piece measures 8" (20.5 cm) from initial CO, with RS facing, use the one-row method (at right) to make a buttonhole over the center 6 sts, knit to end—26 sts rem when all decs have been worked. Work even in St st until piece measures 8" (20.5 cm) from slit, ending with a WS row.

Increase for Sleeves

Use the cable method to CO 2 sts at beg of next 4 rows—34 sts, then CO 4 sts at beg of foll 2 rows—42 sts. Work even until piece measures 11" (28 cm) from slit, ending with a WS row. Work 8 more rows in St st, ending with a WS row—piece measures 13½" (34.5 cm) from slit. Place 14 sts on each of 3 holders.

FRONT

CO and work as for back until piece measures 11" (28 cm) from slit, ending with a WS row—42 sts.

Next row (RS) K20, join a second ball of yarn, BO 2 sts, ssk, knit to end—20 sts rem for left sleeve (as worn) and shoulder; 19 sts rem for right sleeve and shoulder.

Work each side separately as foll:

Right Sleeve and Shoulder

Row 1 (WS) Purl.

Row 2 (RS) K1, ssk, knit to end—1 st dec'd.

Rep Rows 1 and 2 once more—17 sts rem. Work even in St st for 3 rows, ending with a WS row. Place sts on holder.

Left Sleeve and Shoulder

Row 1 (WS) P1, p2tog, purl to end—1 st dec'd.

Row 2 (RS) Knit.

Rep these 2 rows 2 more times—17 sts rem. Work even in St st for 2 rows, ending with a WS row. Place sts on holder.

FINISHING

Place 17 right sleeve and shoulder sts on one needle and the corresponding 14 back sts on another needle. Hold the needles tog so that RS of knitting face tog and use the three-needle method (see Glossary) to BO 13 sts tog from cuff to neck—3 front sts plus 1 back st rem. Rep for other sleeve and shoulder. Place rem 14 back sts on needle along with rem 4 sts from each side—22 sts total.

Hood

With RS facing, rejoin yarn to neck edge. K3, pick up and knit 1 st, k1, pick up and knit 1 st, k7, place marker (pm), k7, pick up and knit 1 st, k1, pick up and knit 1 st, k3—26 sts total. Purl 1 row. Cont as foll:

Row 1 (RS) Knit to 1 st before m, M1R (see Glossary), k1, slip marker (sl m), k1, M1L (see Glossary), knit to end—2 sts inc'd.

Row 2 (WS) Purl.

Rep these 2 rows 11 more times—50 sts. BO all sts.

Seams

Note Crochet seams are worked on the RS to create a decorative ridge. With MC, larger crochet hook, and RS facing, join side seams with single crochet (sc; see Glossary) from sleeve to base of slit (about 22 to 24 sts), inserting hook under just a single strand of each st (not under both strands of each st) leaving 26" (66 cm) open at base for zipper. Join top of hood in a similar manner. Weave in loose ends.

Crochet Trim

With CC, smaller crochet hook, and RS facing, work 4 rnds of sc around hood opening (about 55 sts). Rep for each cuff (about 21 sts around each cuff).

Weave in loose ends. Insert zipper (see Glossary).

ONE-ROW BUTTONHOLE

Bring the yarn to the front of the work, slip the next stitch purlwise, then return the yarn to the back. *Slip the next stitch, pass the second stitch over the slipped stitch (**Figure 1**) and drop it off the needle. Repeat from * 3 more times. Slip the last stitch on the right needle to the left needle and turn the work around. Bring the working yarn to the back, [insert the right needle between the first and second stitches on the left needle (**Figure 2**), draw up a loop and place in on the left needle] 5 times. Turn the work around. With the yarn in back, slip the first stitch and pass the extra cast-on stitch over it (**Figure 3**) and off the needle to complete the buttonhole.

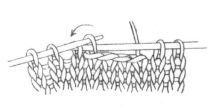

Figure 1

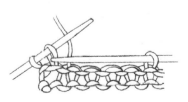

Figure 2

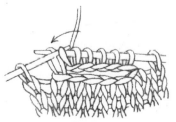

Figure 3

knitter's
DUO

How about knitting a gift for a fellow knitter? **Mags Kandis** has designed a couple of pieces that will be the envy of any knitting group—a roll-up pouch for tape measure, stitch holders, markers, and other essentials, and a caddy to manage up to four separate balls when working colorwork patterns. Both are felted for durability and decorated with a lively splash of free-form embroidery.

FINISHED SIZE *Tool Roll:* About 8¼" (21 cm) wide and 14¼" (36 cm) long with pouch folded, after felting.

Yarn Caddy: About 37" (94 cm) in circumference at top, 26" (66 cm) in circumference at base, and 8" (20.5 cm) tall, after felting.

YARN Fingering weight (#2 Fine) for tool roll; worsted weight (#4 Medium) for yarn caddy.
Shown here: Brown Sheep Nature Spun Fingering Weight (100% wool; 310 yd [283 m]/50 g): #101w burnt sienna (dark rust), 2 balls; #308f sunburst gold, 1 ball.
Brown Sheep Nature Spun Worsted Weight (100% wool; 245 yd [224 m]/100 g): #101w burnt sienna (dark rust) and #308f sunburst gold (gold), 2 balls each.

NEEDLES *Tool roll:* size U.S. 6 (4 mm): straight. *Yarn caddy:* size U.S. 10 (6 mm): straight, 24" (60 cm) circular (cir) and set of 2 double-pointed (dpn). Adjust needle size if necessary to obtain the correct gauge.

NOTIONS Tapestry needle; embroidery needle; marker (m) for yarn caddy only; net laundry bag.

GAUGE *Tool roll:* 21 stitches and 30 rows = 4" (10 cm) with fingering-weight yarn in stockinette stitch on size 6 (4 mm) needles, before felting.

Yarn caddy: 16 stitches and 20 rows = 4" (10 cm) with worsted-weight yarn in stockinette stitch on size 10 (6 mm) needles, before felting.

NOTES
+ In the felting process, the edges of the knitted tool roll may ruffle. To obtain straight sides, simply fold the piece to create the pouch as indicated in the pattern and trim excess material from the sides before stitching into place.

+ When attaching the dividers in the yarn caddy, it may be helpful to baste a straight line from the markers to the beginning of bottom shaping in contrast yarn. Follow this line while stitching.

+ When assembling the yarn caddy, sew with the same color yarn as in the area being attached.

TOOL ROLL

With dark rust, loosely CO 90 sts. Work even in St st until piece measures about 26½" (67.5 cm) from CO. Change to gold and cont in St st until piece measures about 35½" (90 cm) from CO. Loosely BO all sts.

FINISHING

Weave in loose ends.

Felting

Place piece in a net laundry bag. Place the bag and a small amount of mild detergent in the washing machine and run through a cycle set for a small load with a hot wash cycle and a cold rinse cycle. Stop the washer periodically to check the progress of the felting; run through more than one cycle, if necessary, until no individual stitches are visible. Remove from washer and pull into shape—stretching out corners of gold section as desired. Lay flat to dry.

Assembly

Fold up bottom edge of dark rust to produce a pocket 4¾" (12 cm) deep. Trim sides if necessary (see Notes). With dark rust threaded on a tapestry needle, work a blanket stitch (see Glossary) to seam the edges.

Stitching

With dark rust threaded on a tapestry needle, work chain sts (see Glossary) to create free-form circles (beg at the outside and working in toward the center) and "stems" as desired.

Braided Ties

Mark for first tie at center of the pocket edge about ½" (1.3 cm) below top. Cut three lengths of dark rust, each about 20" (51 cm) long. Thread all three lengths tog on a tapestry needle and make a single stitch at the marked position—6 lengths. Center the lengths and divide them into three groups of two strands each. Work a three-strand braid for about 8" (20.5 cm). Tie the end in an overhand knot to secure. Trim ends. Make another braided tie at the center of the pouch, opposite the first tie. Mark for roll tie at center of gold flap about ½" (1.3 cm) from edge. Cut three lengths of gold, each about 60" (152.5 cm) long. Work as for previous braids.

YARN CADDY

With gold and cir needle, loosely CO 152 sts. Place marker (pm) and join for working in rnds, being careful not to twist sts. Work even in St st until piece measures about 6" (15 cm) from CO. Change to dark rust. Cont even in St st until piece measures about 14" (35.5 cm) from CO.

Shape Bottom

Dec Rnd 1 *K17, k2tog; rep from *—144 sts rem.
Knit 1 rnd.
Dec Rnd 2 *K16, k2tog; rep from *—136 sts rem.
Knit 1 rnd.
Dec Rnd 3 *K15, k2tog; rep from *—128 sts rem.
Knit 1 rnd.
Dec Rnd 4 *K14, k2tog; rep from *—120 sts rem.
Knit 1 rnd.
Cont in this manner, working 1 less st between decs every other rnd until 16 sts rem, changing to dpn when there are too few sts to fit comfortably on cir needle.
Next rnd *K2tog; rep from *—8 sts rem.
Knit 1 rnd. Cut yarn, draw tail through rem sts, pull tight, and fasten off on WS.

Dividers (make 2)

With gold and straight needles, loosely CO 62 sts. Work even in St st until piece measures about 6" (15 cm) from CO. Change to dark rust. Cont even in St st until piece measures about 14" (35.5 cm) from CO. Loosely BO all sts.

Handle

With gold and straight needles, loosely CO 56 sts. Knit every row until piece measures about 1½" (3.8 cm) from CO. Loosely BO all sts.

FINISHING

Weave in loose ends. Using contrast waste yarn, mark every 38th st along CO edge of caddy—4 marked sts. With yarn threaded on a tapestry needle (see Notes) and RS of divider pieces facing tog, use backstitches (see Glossary) to sew the two pieces tog at the center to create four equal "wings." Use a whipstitch (see Glossary) to sew the side edges of each divider from marker at CO edge to beg of bottom shaping to form four compartments. Firmly stitch the center point of the divider to the center of the nest bottom, leaving the rem bottom edges free.

Felting

Felt as for tool roll. Lay flat to dry, stretching out the corners of the gold section, as desired.

Stitching

With dark rust threaded on a tapestry needle, work a line of running sts (see Glossary) about ¼" (6 mm) above the top of the dark rust portion of the nest for decoration.

Attach handle to center of divider by firmly stitching in place through all thicknesses.

neckwarmer
HAT

Captivated by the self-striping colors and soft feel of Rowan Tapestry yarn, **Elissa Sugishita** was determined to show it off in a small project. This neck-warmer-cum-hat is a simple tube with ribbing at one end and eyelets to accommodate an I-cord drawstring at the other. Wear it loose around your neck or tighten the cord to close off one end and wear it as a fun hat.

FINISHED SIZE About 24" (61 cm) circumference and 11" (28 cm) tall.

YARN DK weight (#3 Light). *Shown here:* Rowan Tapestry (70% wool, 30% soybean protein fiber; 131 yd [120 m]/50 g): #172 Pot Pourri, 2 balls.

NEEDLES Size U.S. 7 (4.5 mm): 16" (40 cm) circular and set of 2 double-pointed (dpn).

NOTIONS Marker (m); tapestry needle.

GAUGE 21 stitches and 28 rows = 4" (10 cm) in stockinette stitch, worked in rounds.

Eyelet row *K5, k2tog, yo; rep from * to end of rnd.
Cont in St st until piece measures 11" (28 cm) from CO.
Loosely BO all sts.

FINISHING

Weave in loose ends. Block to measurements.

I-Cord

With dpn, CO 3 sts. Work 3-st I-cord (see Glossary) until
piece measures 30" (76 cm) from CO.
Next row K3tog—1 st rem.
Cut yarn, thread tail through rem st, and weave tail to
inside of cord to secure. Thread cord through eyelets. Tie
each end of cord in an overhand knot.

HAT

With cir needle, CO 126 sts. Place marker (pm) and join
for working in rnds, being careful not to twist sts. Work
in k1, p1 rib until piece measures 1½" (3.8 cm) from CO.
Change to St st and work even until piece measures 9"
(23 cm) from CO.

COFFEE CLUTCH

Instead of adding cardboard cup sleeves to the landfill, make a reusable one with leftover bits of yarn. This wool sleeve is worked in a ribbed pattern that tapers to accommodate most sizes of take-out coffee cups. Change colors, add stripes, or incorporate novelty yarns to personalize one for each of your coffee-drinking friends!

Using the long-tail method (see Glossary), CO 48 sts. Arrange sts as evenly as possible on 3 dpn, place marker (pm), and join for working in rnds. Work in k3, p1 rib for 8 rnds.

Inc Rnd 1 *K3, p1, M1 (see Glossary), k3, p1; rep from *—54 sts. Work in k3, p2, k3, p1 rib for 8 rnds.

Inc Rnd 2 *K3, p2, k3, p1, M1; rep from *—60 sts. Work in k3, p2 rib for 8 rnds. Cut yarn, leaving a 28" (71 cm) tail. Thread tail on a tapestry needle and use the sewn method (see Glossary) to BO all sts. Weave in loose ends.

FINISHED SIZE About 7¼" (18.5 cm) circumference at base, 9" (23 cm) circumference at top, and 3¼" (8.5 cm) long.

YARN Worsted weight (#4 Medium).
Shown here: Classic Elite Renaissance (100% wool; 110 yd [110 m]/50 g): #7155 Renaissance red, less than 20 yards.

NEEDLES Size U.S. 5 (3.75 mm): set of 4 or 5 double pointed (dpn). Adjust needle size if necessary to obtain the correct gauge.

NOTIONS Marker (m); tapestry needle.

GAUGE 13 stitches and 18 rounds = 2" (5 cm) in k3, p1 rib, worked in rounds.

felted catnip
MOUSE

The design for **Therese Inverso's** cat toy has its roots in Meg Swansen's knitted (and unfelted) catnip mouse pattern (still available from Schoolhouse Press). Over the years, Therese and her sister, Antonia Young, developed this version with a long "interactive" tail and substantial ears. Halfway through the felting process, the belly is cut open to reveal a cavity that can be filled with a packet of catnip. The rest of the felting process "finishes" the cut edges and prevents raveling. Use leftover bits of yarn and add stripes and decorative stitching as desired to make each mouse individual.

FINISHED SIZE About 7" (18 cm) body circumference, 9" (23 cm) body length, and 32" (81.5 cm) tail length, before felting; about 4¼" (11 cm) body circumference, 6½" (16.5 cm) body length, and 16" (40.5 cm) tail length, after felting.

YARN Worsted weight (#4 Medium).
Shown here: Schoolhouse Press Unspun Icelandic Wool (100% Icelandic wool; 300 yd [274 m]/3½ oz): about 50 yd [46 m] total.

Note The white does not felt as fully as the other colors.

NEEDLES Size U.S. 6 (4 mm): set of 5 double-pointed (dpn). Adjust needle size if necessary to obtain the correct gauge.

NOTIONS Coil-less safety pin; sharp-point tapestry needle; lingerie bag (for felting); 4" by 6" (10 by 15 cm) rectangle of cotton fabric for catnip pouch; small jingle bell (wrapped in fabric to prevent catnip from clogging it); sharp-point sewing needle and matching thread; catnip to fill pouch; contrasting pearl cotton for eyes and whiskers.

GAUGE 20 stitches and 24 rows = 4" (10 cm) in stockinette stitch, worked in rounds.

NOTE
+ Unspun Icelandic wool requires gentle knitting. If the yarn breaks, rejoin it with wet-splicing (see page 44).

TAIL

With CC, CO 4 sts. Work 4-st I-cord (see Glossary) until piece measures about 1" (2.5 cm) from CO. Change to MC (or stripes) and cont in I-cord until piece measures about 30" (76 cm) from CO. Set up for knitting in rnds as foll: [K1f&b] in each st—8 sts total. Divide sts onto 3 dpn (3 sts on each of 2 dpn and 2 sts on 1 dpn) and knit 2 rnds even.

Inc rnd *K1, k1f&b; rep from *—12 sts. Divide sts evenly on 4 dpn (3 sts each needle) and knit 2 rnds even.

Inc rnd *Knit to last st on needle, k1f&b; rep from * 3 more times—4 sts inc'd.

Knit 2 rnds even.

Rep the last 3 rnds 4 more times—32 sts; 8 sts on each needle.

BODY

Cont even until piece measures 2½" (6.5 cm) from last inc rnd.

Neck

Dec 7 sts evenly spaced—25 sts rem. Knit 4 rnds even. Divide sts on 3 dpn so there are 13 sts on the first needle and 6 sts each on the other two needles. Mark the center st on the needle with 13 sts with a coil-less safety pin.

HEAD

Knit to 1 st before marked center st, sl 2 sts tog kwise, k1, p2sso, knit to end of rnd—2 sts dec'd. Dec 2 sts in this manner every 3rd rnd 2 times, then every other rnd 3 times, then every rnd 4 times, adjusting sts on needles as necessary to cont working in rnds—5 sts rem. Cut yarn, leaving a 10" (25.5 cm) tail. Thread tail on tapestry needle so that it is doubled, twist the needle to twist the yarns against each other to strengthen them, then thread it through the rem sts two times, pull tight to close the hole, then work into WS of nose area to add thickness.

Nose

With CC and double strand of yarn (twisted for strength) threaded on a tapestry needle, stitch across the gathered tip to form the nose.

Ears (make 2)

With desired color, CO 5 sts.
Row 1 (WS) [K1, p1] 2 times, k1.
Row 2 [K1, k1f&b] 2 times, k1—7 sts.
Rows 3 and 5 *K1, p1; rep from * to last st, k1.

Row 4 K1, k1f&b, k3, k1f&b, k1—9 sts.
Row 6 Knit.
Rep Rows 5 and 6 four more times. BO all sts. Cut off yarn, leaving a 24" (61 cm) tail. Thread tail on sharp-point tapestry needle. Position the needle at the center point of the tail and twist the needle to "ply" the two strands tog, then use this twisted strand to sew the ear to the side of the face.

FINISHING

Reinforce the tail by running several strands of doubled, twisted yarn along the center of the I-cord tube. To strengthen the base of the tail, work a couple of rows of duplicate sts (see Glossary) with doubled yarn at the base of the tail.

Felting

Place the mouse in a lingerie bag to keep the tail from being tangled in the washing machine. Felt the mouse according to instructions for the Oven Mitt on page 44 until the piece is about halfway felted. Carefully cut a slit along the base of the belly from the neck to the tail. Gently stuff the face to the tip of the nose with some wool lint (use what you retrieved from the washer during the early stages of felting) to prevent the face from felting tog. (The rest of the stuffing is added during assembly.) Tug on the tail to make sure it felts evenly and cont felting as for the Oven Mitts.

Catnip Pouch

Fold the pouch fabric in half lengthwise and hand- or machine-stitch the side and bottom tog. Stuff with catnip and a fabric-wrapped bell, then sew the top closed.

Assembly

Stuff the head and tail taper of the dry mouse firmly with yarn scraps or wool lint. Insert the catnip pouch in the body cavity, then use doubled, twisted yarn to tightly sew the cavity closed. With about 12" (30.5 cm) of pearl cotton threaded on a sharp-point needle, make 2 French knots (see Glossary) for eyes, then add whiskers at tip of nose.

evening
LACE

Shawls make great wraps when the temperatures drop. But they can fall off the shoulders and be awkward to wear when you need to have both arms and hands free. **Cecily Glowik MacDonald** solved the problem with this lacy little top that's more vest than shawl. It is worked in a single piece from the lower back to the neck, then the fronts are split into two halves that are worked down to the lower front edge. The fronts and back are seamed at the sides, and it's ready to wear!

FINISHED SIZE About 34 (39½, 47, 52½, 57½)" (86.5 [99.5, 119.5, 133.5, 146] cm) bust circumference, relaxed after blocking. Top shown measures 34" (86.5 cm).

YARN Worsted weight (#4 Medium).
Shown here: FibraNatura Mermaid (42% cotton, 35% superwash merino, 12% silk, 11% seacell; 125 yd [114.5 m]/50 g): #40603 purple, 4 (5, 5, 6, 6) balls.

NEEDLES Size U.S. 8 (5 mm). Adjust needle size if necessary to obtain the correct gauge.

NOTIONS Tapestry needle.

GAUGE 18½ stitches and 20 rows = 4" (10 cm) in lace pattern, relaxed after blocking.

stitch guide

BODY

CO 78 (90, 108, 120, 132) sts. Work in k3, p3 rib (see
Stitch Guide) until piece measures ¾" (2 cm) or desired
length from CO, ending with a WS row.

Next row (RS) Work Row 1 of lace patt (see Stitch Guide)
across all sts.

Cont in lace patt until piece measures about 15 (15, 15, 16,
16)" (38 [38, 38, 40.5, 40.5] cm) from CO, ending with a WS
row. **Note** Because the lace patt is stretchy, stretch the piece
to the correct width before measuring.

Divide for Back and Fronts

With RS facing and cont in patt, work 30 (36, 42, 48, 54)
sts, join a second ball of yarn and BO 18 (18, 24, 24, 24) sts
in patt for neck, work to end—30 (36, 42, 48, 54) sts rem
for each front.

Fronts

Working each side separately, cont as established until each
piece measures 16¼ (16¼, 16¼, 17¼, 17¼)" (41.5 [41.5,
41.5, 44, 44] cm) or desired length from BO row, ending
with a WS row. **Note** One center front ends with p3; the
other center front begins with k3. Work in k3, p3 rib for ¾"
(2 cm). Loosely BO all sts in rib patt.

FINISHING

Block piece to measurements. Weave in loose ends. With
yarn threaded on a tapestry needle, sew side seams for 6½"
(16.5 cm), starting at CO edge and leaving rem 9½ (9½,
9½, 10½, 10½)" (24 [24, 24, 26.5, 26.5] cm) open below
shoulder for armhole.

BOBBLE BOOKMARKS

Mags Kandis once gifted me a nifty bookmark made from a colorful crochet flower at the end of a three-stand braid. In this version, three knitted bobbles are tied together in an overhand knot, then the ends are braided and secured with another overhand knot. Mix and match leftover bits of yarn to suit your favorite reader's personality.

Leaving a tail about 26" (66 cm) long, make a slipknot and place on needle. [K1f&b] 3 times—6 sts. Work even in St st (knit RS rows; purl WS rows) for 6 rows. Pass the second, third, fourth, fifth, and sixth sts over the first st—1 st. Cut yarn, leaving a 26" (66 cm) tail. Tie the CO and BO tails tog in a square knot to shape the bobble.

Make two more bobbles the same way.

Tie three bobbles in a cluster by tying the tails in an overhand knot close to the bobbles. Hold the bobble cluster steady (tape them to a tabletop or close them in a drawer) and working the two tails from each bobble as a unit, work a three-strand braid for about 10" (25.5 cm) or desired length. Tie another overhand knot to secure the ends. Trim close to the knot.

FINISHED SIZE About 10" (25.5 cm) long.

YARN Sportweight (#2 Fine). *Shown here:* Louet North America Gems Sport Weight (100% merino; 225 yd [206 m]/100 g): a few yards. Shown in mustard, terra-cotta, and grape.

NEEDLES Size U.S. 3 (3.25 mm).

NOTIONS Tapestry needle.

GAUGE Gauge is not important for this project.

winter sky

HAT & MITTENS

*T*o give a little asymmetric interest to an otherwise plain toque-style hat, **Judith L. Swartz** added an intertwined cable panel punctuated with bobbles. The hat begins with a few rounds of garter stitch and ends with a chunky tassel that causes the top to fold over at a jaunty angle. The matching mittens feature the same decorative panel along the back of the hands. Knitted with the softest merino yarn, these pieces are warm and never scratchy.

FINISHED SIZE *Hat:* About 17 (19, 21)" (43 [48.5, 53.5] cm) circumference and 9 (10, 10)" (23 [25.5, 25.5] cm) long. To fit child's large/adult small (adult medium, adult large). Hat shown measures 19" (48.5 cm) circumference.

Mittens: About 7 (8, 9)" (18 [20.5, 23] cm) circumference and 9 (10, 10)" (23 [25.5, 25.5] cm) long. To fit child's large/adult small (adult medium, adult large). Mittens shown measure 8" (20.5 cm) circumference.

YARN Worsted weight (#4 Medium).
Shown here. Morehouse Farms Merino 3-Strand Worsted (100% merino; 140 yd [128 m]/2 oz): sky (pale blue), 2 (2, 3) skeins.

NEEDLES Size 9 (5.5 mm): 16" (40 cm) circular (cir) and set of 4 double-pointed (dpn). Adjust needle size if necessary to obtain the correct gauge.

NOTIONS Markers (m); cable needle (cn); small stitch holder or waste yarn; tapestry needle; 4" (10 cm) square of cardboard for making tassel.

GAUGE 16 stitches and 24 rounds = 4" (10 cm) in stockinette stitch, worked in rounds.

+ **MB (make bobble)**
Knit into the front, back, front, back, and front of next st—5 sts made from 1. Pass the fourth, third, second, first sts over the fifth and off the needle—1 st rem.

+ **C3B (cross three back)**
Slip 1 st onto cn and hold in back of work, k2, p1 from cn.

+ **C3F (cross three front)**
Sl 2 sts onto cn and hold in front of work, p1, k2 from cn.

+ **C5BP (cross 5 back purl)**
Sl 3 sts onto cn and hold in back of work, k2, (p1, k2) from cn.

+ **BOBBLED CABLE PATT (panel of 9 sts)**
Rnd 1 P1, C3B (see above), p1, C3F (see above), p1.
Rnds 2 and 8 P1, k2, p3, k2, p1.
Rnd 3 C3B, p3, C3F.
Rnds 4 and 6 K2, p5, k2.
Rnd 5 K2, p2, MB (see above), p2, k2.
Rnd 7 C3F, p3, C3B.
Rnd 9 P1, C3F, p1, C3B, p1.
Rnd 10 P2, k5, p2.
Rnd 11 P2, C5BP (see above), p2.
Rnd 12 P2, k5, p2.
Repeat Rnds 1–12 for pattern.

HAT

With dpn or cir needle, CO 73 (81, 89) sts. Place marker (pm) and join for working in rnds, being careful not to twist sts. Purl 1 rnd, knit 1 rnd, purl 1 rnd.

Set-up rnd K32 (36, 40), pm, work Rnd 1 of bobbled cable patt (see Stitch Guide) over next 9 sts, pm, knit to end of rnd.

Work even in patt until piece measures about 5 (6, 6)" (12.5 [15, 15] cm) from CO.

Shape Top

Note If using cir needle, change to dpn when there are too few sts to fit comfortably on cir needle.

Dec rnd [Ssk, k6 (7, 8), pm] 4 times, work next 9 sts in cable patt, [k6 (7, 8), k2tog, pm] 4 times—8 sts dec'd.

Work 3 rnds even.

Dec rnd [Ssk, knit to m, sl m] 4 times, work next 9 sts in cable patt, [knit to 2 sts before next m, k2tog, sl m] 4 times—8 sts dec'd.

Dec 8 sts in this manner every 4th rnd once more, then every other rnd 4 (5, 6) more times—17 sts rem. Work 1 rnd even.

Next rnd Removing markers as you go, [ssk] 2 times, work cable panel, [k2tog] 2 times—13 sts rem.

Work 1 rnd even.

Next rnd K2tog, work cable panel, ssk—11 sts rem.

Cut yarn, leaving a 6" (15 cm) tail. Thread tail through tapestry needle and draw it through rem 11 sts. Gently pull yarn tail to close top of hat, then fasten it to the WS.

FINISHING

Make a tassel as decribed (at right). Weave in loose ends. Block lightly.

RIGHT MITTEN

With dpn, CO 35 (39, 43) sts. Divide sts among 3 dpn as foll: 19 (21, 23) sts on Needle 1 and 8 (9, 10) sts each on Needle 2 and Needle 3. Place marker (pm) and join for working in rnds, being careful not to twist sts. Purl 1 rnd, knit 1 rnd, purl 1 rnd.

Set-up rnd On Needle 1, K5 (6, 7), pm, work Rnd 1 of bobbled cable patt (see Stitch Guide) over next 9 sts, pm, k5 (6, 7); on Needle 2, Knit; on Needle 3, knit.

Cont in patt as established until piece measures 2" (5 cm) from CO (about 1 full patt rep).

Thumb Gusset

Keeping in patt, work 18 (20, 22) sts, pm, M1 (see Glossary), k2, M1, pm, work to end of rnd—4 gusset sts between markers.

Work 1 rnd even.

Next rnd Work to m, slip marker (sl m), M1, knit to next m, M1, sl m (6 gusset sts between markers), work to end.

Rep last 2 rnds until there are 10 (12, 12) gusset sts between markers. Work 6 rnds even.

Next rnd Work to m, remove m, k10 (12, 12) gusset sts, remove m, place 10 (12, 12) gusset sts just worked onto holder or waste yarn, work to end of rnd.

On the next rnd, use the backward-loop method (see Glos-

TASSEL

Cut a piece of cardboard 4" (10 cm) wide by the desired length of the tassel plus 1" (2.5 cm). Wrap yarn to desired thickness around cardboard. Cut a short length of yarn and tie tightly around one end of wrapped yarn (Figure 1). Cut yarn loops at other end. Cut another piece of yarn and wrap tightly around loops a short distance below top knot to form tassel neck. Knot securely, thread ends onto tapestry needle, and pull to center of tassel (Figure 2). Trim ends.

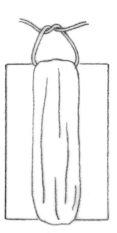

Figure 1

Figure 2

sary) to CO 2 sts over gap formed by held gusset sts—35 (39, 43) sts. Adjust sts, if necessary, so that there are 19 (21, 23) sts on Needle 1 and 8 (9, 10) sts each on Needle 2 and Needle 3. Cont even in patt until piece measures 8 (9, 10)" (20.5 [23, 25.5] cm) from CO.

Shape Top

Dec as foll: On Needle 1, ssk, work in patt to last 2 sts, k2tog; on Needle 2, knit; on Needle 3, knit—33 (37, 41) sts rem. Work 1 rnd even.

Next rnd On Needle 1, ssk, work in patt to last 2 sts, k2tog; on Needle 2, ssk, knit to end; on Needle 3, knit to last 2 sts, k2tog—4 sts dec'd.

Rep the last 2 rnds 5 more times (12 rnds total)—9 (13, 17) sts rem; 5 (7, 9) sts on Needle 1 and 2 (3, 4) sts each on Needle 2 and Needle 3.

Next rnd Keeping in patt, dec 1 st at center of cable—8 (12, 16) sts rem; 4 (6, 8) sts on Needle 1 and 2 (3, 4) sts each on Needle 2 and Needle 3.

Slip the sts from Needle 3 onto Needle 2—4 (6, 8) sts each on 2 needles. Cut yarn, leaving a 10" (25.5 cm) tail. Thread tail on a tapestry needle and use the Kitchener st (see Glossary) to graft the sts tog.

Thumb

Place 10 (12, 12) held gusset sts evenly spaced on 2 dpn. Join yarn to beg of these sts, k10 (12, 12), then use a third needle to pick up and knit 4 sts evenly spaced at base of CO sts—14 (16, 16) sts total; 5 (6, 6) sts each on Needle 1 and Needle 2, 4 sts on Needle 3. Join for working in rnds and knit every rnd until piece measures 1¾ (2, 2½)" (4.5 [5, 6.5] cm) from pick-up rnd.

Next rnd K1, *k2tog, k1; rep from *, working any extra sts as k1—10 (11, 11) sts rem.

Work 1 rnd even.

Next rnd *K2tog; rep from *, end k0 (1, 1)—5 (6, 6) sts rem. Knit 1 rnd. Cut yarn, leaving a 6" (15 cm) tail. Thread tail on tapestry needle, draw it through rem sts, pull tight to close hole, and fasten off on WS.

LEFT MITTEN

With dpn, CO 35 (39, 43) sts. Divide sts among 3 dpn as foll: 8 (9, 10) sts each on Needle 1 and Needle 2 and 19 (21, 23) sts on Needle 3. Pm and join for working in rnds, being careful not to twist sts. Purl 1 rnd, knit 1 rnd, purl 1 rnd.

Set-up rnd On Needle 1, knit; on Needle 2, knit; on Needle 3, k5 (6, 7), pm, work Rnd 1 of bobbled cable patt over next 9 sts, pm, k5 (6, 7).

Cont in patt as established until piece measures 2" (5 cm) from CO (about 1 full patt rep).

Thumb Gusset

Keeping in patt, work 15 (17, 19) sts, pm, M1, k2, M1, pm, work to end of rnd—2 gusset sts inc'd; 4 gusset sts between markers. Work 1 rnd even.

Next rnd Work to m, slip marker (sl m), M1, knit to next m, M1, sl m, work to end.

Rep last 2 rnds until there are 10 (12, 12) gusset sts between markers. Work 6 rnds even.

Next rnd Work to m, remove m, k10 (12, 12) gusset sts, remove m, place 10 (12, 12) gusset sts just worked onto holder or waste yarn, work to end of rnd.

On the next rnd, use the backward-loop method to CO 2 sts over gap formed by held gusset sts—35 (39, 43) sts. Adjust sts, if necessary, so there are 8 (9, 10) sts each on Needle 1 and Needle 2 and 19 (21, 23) sts on Needle 3. Cont even in patt until piece measures 8 (9, 10)" (20.5 [23, 25.5] cm) from CO.

Shape Top

Dec as foll: On Needle 1, knit; on Needle 2, knit; on Needle 3, ssk, work in patt to last 2 sts, k2tog—33 (37, 41) sts rem. Cont as for right mitten.

Thumb

Work as for right mitten.

FINISHING

Weave in loose ends. Block lightly.

sugar
&spice
BLANKET

To keep her busy while she eagerly anticipated the arrival of her first granddaughter, **JoLene Treace** knitted a blanket that could be passed down to the next generation. JoLene found the simple eyelet and garter-stitch pattern in a Japanese book of stitch patterns. She added a saw-tooth edging that complements the stitch pattern and tied the design together with harmonious balance. The yarn, a superwash merino, is soft as a whisper and easy to launder.

FINISHED SIZE 40" (101.5 cm) square.

YARN Fingering weight (#1 Super Fine).
Shown here: Filatura di Crosa Zarina (100% merino superwash; 180 yd [165 m]/50 g): #1462 pale blue, 9 balls.

NEEDLES Size U.S. 2 (3 mm): 32" (80 cm) circular (cir) and one 7" (18 cm) double-pointed (dpn). Adjust needle size if necessary to obtain the correct gauge.

NOTIONS Markers (m); tapestry needle.

GAUGE 24 stitches and 40 rows = 4" (10 cm) in blanket pattern, blocked with moderate stretch.

NOTES
+ A slipped (chain) selvedge stitch is worked at each edge to facilitate attaching edging as it is worked.

+ The garter-stitch border and edging are worked on a purled garter-stitch ground—purl right- and wrong-side rows.

+ Each 12-row pattern repeat of the edging forms a "point."

+ When working the edging, right-side (odd-numbered) rows are worked away from the blanket; wrong-side (even-numbered) rows are worked toward the blanket.

stitch guide

BLANKET

With cir needle and using the knitted method (see Glossary), CO 231 sts. Do not join.

Bottom Border

Working the first and last st of each row as a slipped (chain) selvedge (see Notes), purl 6 rows.

Body

Work 4 sts as established for side border, place marker (pm), work center 223 sts according to Row 1 of Body chart, pm, work 4 sts as established for side border. Cont as established, work through Row 10 of chart, then rep Rows 1–10 of chart 36 more times—37 repeats total. Work Rows 1–6 once more—piece measures about 32" (81.5 cm) from beg of charted patt.

Top Border

Working the first and last st as slipped selvedge, purl 6 rows, ending with a WS row.

Edging

Set-up rnd (RS) P2, *p2tog, p5; rep from * to last 5 sts, p2tog, p3—198 sts rem.
Pm and pick up and purl (see Glossary) 198 sts along left edge of body as foll: Pick up and purl into front and back leg of each of the first 5 selvedge chain sts, pick up and purl into front leg only of every selvedge st to the last 4 sts, pick up and purl into front and back loop of each of the last 4 selvedge sts, pm, cont across bottom border of blanket, cont across 198 sts of top border, pm, pick up and purl 198 sts along right edge of body as foll: Pick up and purl into front and back leg of each of the first 5 selvedge chain sts, pick up and purl into front leg only of every selvedge st to the last 4 sts, pick up and purl into front and back loop of each of the last 4 selvedge sts—792 sts total. Cut yarn, leaving an 8" (20.5 cm) tail for finishing later.

Work edging (see Notes) while attaching it to the blanket as foll: With dpn, CO 5 sts. Purl to last st, sl the last st onto the left-hand tip of the cir needle with the WS of the blanket facing, and purl it tog with the first st on the cir needle. Turn work. Work Row 1 of Edging chart. Cont in patt, work the last st of edging tog with next st of blanket every WS row, working 33 points along each side of the blanket (132 points total)—5 edging sts rem. BO all sts.

FINISHING

With yarn threaded on a tapestry needle, use a whipstitch (see Glossary) to join the CO and BO edges of the edging. Weave in loose ends. Wash the blanket in wool wash or mild detergent, blot excess moisture with towels. Place damp blanket on a flat surface and pin the points to form a 40" (101.5 cm) square. Allow to thoroughly air-dry before removing pins.

Body

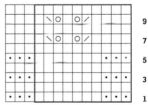

Side border sts not shown on chart

Edging

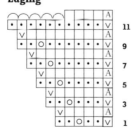

	knit on RS; purl on WS
•	purl on RS; knit on WS
/	k2tog on RS
\	ssk on RS
V	sl 1 st purlwise
O	yarnover (YO)
Λ	attach edging: p2tog using last edging st and first st held on left needle
⌒	BO
	pattern repeat

ulla's
SCARF

$\mathcal{N}$ ancy Bush used traditional Estonian techniques in this exquisite scarf—a scalloped edging, garter-stitch borders, and a stunning lace pattern, called *piibelehtkiri* (lily of the valley). The scarf begins at one end with a scalloped edging, the body of the scarf is worked to the other end, then a separate scalloped edging is worked and grafted in place—all with a single skein of yarn. Nancy named this scarf for Ulla Kaljurand—a good friend who helped Nancy research Estonian knitting and shared her culture, cuisine, and lovely garden during Nancy's visits.

FINISHED SIZE About 6" (15 cm) wide and 55" (139.5 cm) long, after blocking.

YARN Fingering weight (#1 Super Fine).
Shown here: Tools Le Blanc 60/40 Merino Angora "Fingering"

(60% merino, 40% angora; 250 yd [228 m]/2 oz): tort, 1 skein (with no yarn left over).

NEEDLES Size U.S. 5 (3.75 mm). Adjust needle size if necessary to obtain the correct gauge.

NOTIONS Tapestry needle.

GAUGE 10 stitches and 14 rows = 2" (5 cm) in stockinette stitch, before blocking.

SCARF
Bottom Lace Edging

With two strands of yarn held tog and using the knitted method (see Glossary), CO 31 sts. Break off one strand of yarn and cont with single strand only. Knit 2 rows. Work Rows 1–12 of Lace Edge chart. Slipping the first st of every row purlwise with yarn in front (pwise wyf), knit 6 rows (3 garter ridges), ending with a WS row.

Center Section

(RS) Sl 1 pwise wyf, k4, place marker (pm), work Row 1 of Center chart across 21 sts, pm, k5.

Next row (WS) Sl 1 pwise wyf, k4, slip marker (sl m), purl to m, sl m, k5.

Slipping the first st of every row pwise wyf and working the next 4 sts and the last 5 sts in garter st (not shown on chart), work through Row 28 of chart, then rep Rows 1–28 ten more times, then work Rows 1–14 once more—piece measures about 51½" (131 cm) from CO; 322 rows total. Slipping the first st of every row pwise wyf, knit 4 rows (2 garter ridges). Break yarn, leaving an 8" (20.5 cm) tail. Set aside.

Top Lace Edging

With two strands of yarn held tog and using the knitted method, CO 31 sts. Break off one strand of yarn and cont with single strand only. Knit 2 rows (do not slip the first st of every row). Work Rows 1–12 of Lace Edge chart. Slipping the first st of every row pwise wyf, knit 2 rows. Break yarn, leaving a 20" (51 cm) tail for grafting.

FINISHING

Place sts for center section on a needle. Hold the center section and top lace edging tog so that RS are facing up. Thread the longer tail on a tapestry needle and use the Kitchener st (see Glossary) to graft the two pieces tog, matching the tension of the knitted sts.

Handwash gently in mild soap and warm water. Pin scarf out to desired shape. When dry, weave in loose ends.

Center Lace

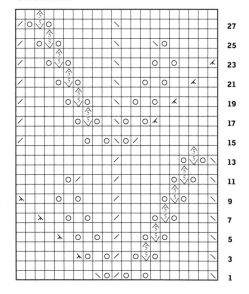

Lace Edge

Work sts between markers 2 times

□	knit on RS; purl on WS.
·	purl on RS; knit on WS.
5	nupp—(k1, yo, k1, yo, k1) into 1 st on RS row.
5	p5tog on WS row to complete nupp.
\	sl 1, k1, psso
/	k2tog
O	yarnover (yo)
⅄	sl 1, k2tog, psso
∠	k3tog
□	pattern repeat
↓	marker

shaadi
MITTS

*I*nspired by the tradition of Indian brides to decorate their hands with henna patterns and (in North India) wear a lattice of gold chains and medallions, **Jaya Srikrishnan** designed these intricately patterned fingerless mitts. The backs of the hands are worked in a traditional stranded knitting pattern that mimics the *mehndi* (henna) pattern and the palms are worked in a Bavarian twisted stitch pattern that resembles the gold chains. These mitts are a bit challenging to knit, but they'll last a lot longer than a henna tattoo.

FINISHED SIZE About 7 (7¾, 8½)" (18 [19.5, 21.5] cm) circumference and 7 (7½, 8)" (18 [19, 20.5] cm) long. Mitts shown measure 7" (18 cm) in circumference.

YARN Fingering weight (#1 Super Fine).
Shown here: Lorna's Laces Shepherd Sock (100% superwash merino; 215 yd [195 m]/50 g): #37ns violet (A) and #107 red rover (B), 1 skein each.

NEEDLES Size U.S. 1 (2.25 mm): set of 5 double-point (dpn). Adjust needle size if necessary to obtain the correct gauge.

NOTIONS Split-ring or removable markers (m); cable needle (cn); smooth cotton waste yarn; tapestry needle.

GAUGE 34 stitches = 2¾" (7 cm) in charted twisted stitch pattern; 34 stitches = 3" (7.5 cm) in charted colorwork pattern; 45 rounds = 4⅛" (10.5 cm) in all charted patterns.

NOTES
+ Stretch the stitches on the right needle when changing colors to ensure that the floats are loose enough.

+ Catch the stranded yarn on the wrong side every 3 stitches or so to prevent long floats—this will allow the color to peek through the front and create the heathered effect. Change the location of where the stranded yarn is caught to prevent vertical lines.

RIGHT HAND

With A, CO 80 (88, 96) sts. Divide sts, placing 34 sts each on Needles 1 and 3 and 6 (10, 14) sts each on Needles 2 and 4. Attach split-ring marker (pm) into the last st at the end of each needle. Join for working in rnds, being careful not to twist sts.

Cuff

Set-up rnd On Needles 1 and 3, k1, *p2, [k2, p2] 2 times, k1; rep from * 2 times, pm (see Notes); on Needles 2 and 4, [p2, k2] 1 (2, 3) time(s), p2, pm. Work sts as they appear (knit the knits and purl the purl for 29 more rnds (30 rnds total) or until piece measures desired length to base of thumb.

Thumb Gusset

Join B and work Rnd 1 of Palm chart across 34 sts for palm, slip marker (sl m), k6 (10, 14) with A, sl m, work Rnd 1 of Right Back of Hand chart across 34 sts for back of hand, sl m, k3 (5, 7) with A, pm, use the backward-loop method (see Glossary) to CO 1 st for gusset (this st represents Rnd 1 of Gusset chart), pm, k3 (5, 7) with A. Cont working charts as established through Rnd 24 of Gusset chart—21 gusset sts between markers. (**Note** For a longer gusset, cont in checkerboard patt as established while working Palm and Right Back of Hand charts to the desired length.) Place 21 gusset sts plus 1 (2, 3) st(s) on each side of gusset on waste yarn holder, removing thumb gusset markers—23 (25, 27) gusset sts on holder; 78 (84, 90) sts rem for hand.

Hand

Work Palm chart across 34 sts, sl m, k6 (10, 14) with A, sl m, work Right Back of Hand chart across 34 sts, sl m, k2 (3, 4) with A, over gap formed by held sts, use the backward-loop method to CO 2 (4, 6) sts with A, k2 (3, 4) with A—80 (88, 96) sts. Cont in patts as established

Left Back of Hand

Gusset

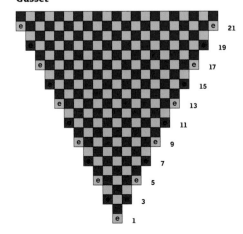

Right Back of Hand

Palm

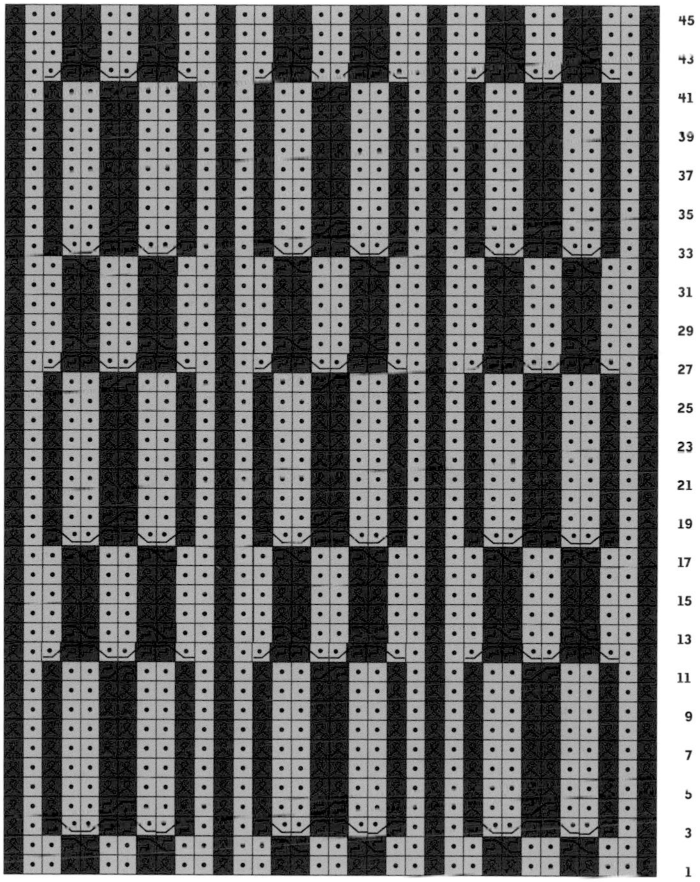

	Color A—knit on RS
	Color A—purl on RS
	Color B—knit on RS
e	increase 1 st using e-wrap (backward loop CO method) and Color A
	increase 1 st using e-wrap and Color B
	knit 1 st through back loop with Color B

Right Twist—K: sl next st from left needle onto cn, hold in back of work; with color B, k1tbl from left needle, then k1 tbl from cn with color B.

Left Twist—K: sl next st from left needle onto cn, hold in front of work; with color B, k1tbl from left needle, then k1tbl from cn with color B.

Right Twist—K & P: sl next st from left needle onto cn, hold in back; with color B, k1tbl from left needle, then p1 from cn with color A

Left Twist—P & K: sl next st from left needle onto cn, hold in front; with color A, p1 from left needle, then k1tbl from cn with color B.

through Rnd 45 of charts. Cut off B. With A only, work rib patt as for cuff until piece measures 7 (7½, 8)" (18 [19, 20.5] cm) from CO. BO all sts in patt.

Thumb

Place 23 (25, 27) held gusset sts on needles. With A, pick up and knit 2 (4, 6) sts along base of CO sts (see Notes), knit to last st, k2tog (last st and first picked-up st), pm, and join for working in rnds—24 (28, 32) sts. Work in k2, p2 rib for 7 (8, 9) rnds or until thumb measures desired length. BO all sts in patt.

LEFT HAND

CO and work cuff as for right hand.

Thumb Gusset

Join B and work Rnd 1 of Left Back of Hand chart across 34 sts for back of hand, sl m, k6 (10, 14) with A, sl m, work Rnd 1 of Palm chart across 34 sts for palm, sl m, k3 (5, 7) with A, pm, use the backward-loop method to CO 1 st for gusset (this st represents Rnd 1 of Gusset chart), pm, k3

(5, 7) with A. Cont working charts as established through Rnd 24 of Gusset chart—21 gusset sts between markers, or for same length of right-hand gusset. Place 21 gusset sts plus 1 (2, 3) sts on each side of gusset on waste yarn holder, removing thumb gusset markers—23 (25, 27) gusset sts on holder; 78 (84, 90) sts rem for hand.

Hand

Work Left Back of Hand chart across 34 sts, sl m, k6 (10, 14) with A, sl m, work Palm chart across 34 sts, sl m, k2 (3, 4) with A, use the backward-loop method to CO 2 (4, 6) sts with A, k2 (3, 4) with A—80 (88, 96) sts. Cont in patts as established through Rnd 45 of charts. Cut off B. With A only, work rib patt as for cuff until piece measures 7 (7½, 8)" (18 [19, 20.5] cm) from CO. BO all sts in patt.

Thumb

Work thumb as for right hand.

FINISHING

Weave in loose ends. Block lightly.

RUFFLED BOTTLE SLEEVE

Protect your table from wine drips with a ruffled sleeve (and use up some leftover yarn in the process). This flexible sleeve is worked in a rib pattern that hugs the wine bottle. The ruffle at the bottom adds just a bit of whimsy. Add beads, appliqués, or embroidery to fit any occasion.

Using the long-tail method (see Glossary), CO 32 sts. Divide sts evenly on 4 dpn, place marker (pm), and join for working in rnds, being careful not to twist sts. Work in k3, p1 rib until piece measures about 2¾" (7 cm) from CO, or desired length to beg of ruffle.

Inc Rnd 1 [K1f&b] 32 times—64 sts.

Inc Rnd 2 [K1f&b] 64 times—128 sts.

BO all sts.

Weave in loose ends.

FINISHED SIZE About 3" (7.5 cm) in circumference and 3" (7.5 cm) long.

YARN Fingering weight (#1 Super Fine).
Shown here: Lorna's Laces Shepherd Sock (100% superwash merino; 215 yd [195 m]/50 g): about 10 yards. Shown in #107 red rover.

NEEDLES Size U.S. 2 (2.75 mm): set of 5 double-pointed (dpn). Adjust needle size if necessary to obtain the correct gauge.

NOTIONS Marker (m); tapestry needle.

GAUGE 21 stitches and 24 rounds = 2" (5 cm) in k3, p1 rib, worked in rounds.

his & her
SOCKS

Handknitted socks are always a welcome gift. The patterns on these socks are simple combinations of knit and purl stitches that are interchangeable and easy to modify into other variations. The socks shown here are knitted with machine-washable sportweight merino yarn that is warm and never scratchy. They are worked at a tight gauge that is more typical for fingering-weight yarn to produce a dense well-wearing fabric. Make a pair for everyone in the family!

FINISHED SIZE About 6½ (7, 8)" (16.5 [10, 20.5] cm) foot circumference with rib slightly stretched, 7 (8½, 10)" (18 [21.5, 25.5] cm) foot length from back of heel to tip of toe, and 9 (10¼, 10¼)" (23 [26, 26] cm) leg length from base of heel to top of cuff. To fit a child (woman, man). Blue socks shown measure 7" (18 cm) foot circumference; brown socks shown measure 8" (20.5 cm) foot circumference.

YARN Sportweight (#2 Fine). *Shown here:* Louet North America Gems Sport Weight (100% merino; 225 yd [206 m]/100 g): 1 (2, 2) skeins. Shown in French blue and ginger.

NEEDLES Size U.S. 2 (2.75 mm): set of 4 double-pointed (dpn). Adjust needle size if necessary to obtain the correct gauge.

NOTIONS Marker (m); tapestry needle.

GAUGE 16 stitches and 22 rounds = 2" (5 cm) in stockinette stitch, worked in rounds.

stitch guide

+ CUFF PATTERN (multiple of 4 sts)
Rnds 1 and 3 Knit.
Rnds 2 and 4 Purl.
Rnds 5, 6, and 7 *K2, p2; rep from *.
Rnd 8 Purl.
Repeat Rnds 5–8 (do not rep Rnds 1–4)
two more times.

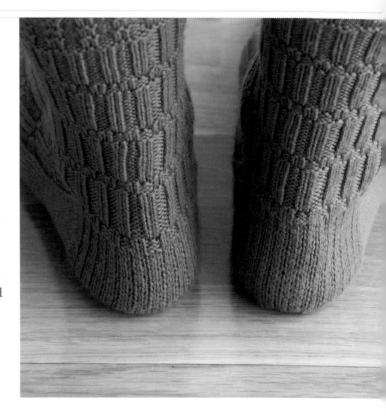

LEG

CO 52 (60, 68) sts. Place marker (pm) and join for working
in rnds, being careful not to twist sts. Work 16 rnds of cuff
patt (see Stitch Guide). Choose between Checkerboard Rib
and Broken Rib charts and work in chosen patt until piece
measures about 6 (7¼, 7¼)" (15 [18.5, 18.5] cm) or desired
length from CO, ending with Rnd 12 or 15 of Checkerboard
Rib chart or Rnd 15, 19, or 23 of Broken Rib chart.

HEEL

Divide for heel as foll: K13 (15, 17), turn work.
Next row (WS) Sl 1, p25 (29, 33)—26 (30, 34) heel sts on
  one needle.
Rearrange sts if necessary so that heel sts begin and end
with k2 or p2 to ensure that patt is centered on instep.
Arrange rem 26 (30, 34) instep sts between 2 needles to
work later.

Heel Flap

Work 26 (30, 34) heel sts back and forth in rows as foll:
Row 1 (RS) *Sl 1 pwise with yarn in back (wyb), k1; rep
  from *.
Row 2 (WS) Sl 1 pwise with yarn in front (wyf), purl to end.
Rep Rows 1 and 2 until a total of 26 (30, 34) rows have
been worked—13 (15, 17) chain sts along each selvedge
edge.

Turn Heel

Work short-rows as foll:
Row 1 (RS) Sl 1 pwise wyb, k14 (16, 18), ssk, k1, turn work.

Row 2 (WS) Sl 1 pwise wyf, p5, p2tog, p1, turn work.
Row 3 Sl 1 pwise wyb, knit to 1 st before gap formed on
  previous row, ssk (1 st each side of gap), k1, turn work.
Row 4 Sl 1 pwise wyf, purl to 1 st before gap formed on
  previous row, p2tog (1 st each side of gap), p1, turn
  work.
Rep Rows 3 and 4 until all heel sts have been worked,
ending with a WS row—16 (18, 20) heel sts rem.

Gussets

Pick up sts along selvedge edges of heel flap and rejoin for
working in rnds as foll:
Rnd 1 With Needle 1, sl 1, k15 (17, 19) to end of heel sts,
  then pick up and knit 13 (15, 17) sts along selvedge
  edge of heel flap; with Needle 2, k26 (30, 34) instep in
  patt as established; with Needle 3, pick up and knit 13

(15, 17) sts along other selvedge edge of heel flap, then knit 8 (9, 10) heel sts from Needle 1—68 (78, 88) sts. Rnd begins at back of heel.

Rnd 2 On Needle 1, knit to last 2 sts, k2tog; on Needle 2, work instep sts in patt; on Needle 3, ssk, knit to end—2 sts dec'd.

Rnd 3 Knit.

Rep Rnds 2 and 3 until 52 (60, 68) sts rem—13 (15, 17) sts each on Needle 1 and Needle 3; 26 (30, 34) sts on Needle 2.

FOOT

Working instep sts in patt and bottom-of-foot sts in St st, work even until foot measures about 5½ (6¾, 8)" (14 [17, 20.5] cm) from back of heel or about 1½ (1¾, 2)" (3.8 [4.5, 5] cm) less than desired total length, ending with a purl row if working broken rib patt and working this row across all instep sts for a decorative ridge.

Toe

Dec at each side of foot as foll:

Rnd 1 On Needle 1, knit to last 3 sts, k2tog, k1; on Needle 2, k1, ssk, knit to last 3 sts, k2tog, k1; on Needle 3, k1, ssk, knit to end—4 sts dec'd.

Rnd 2 Knit.

Rep Rnds 1 and 2 until 28 (32, 36) sts rem, then rep Rnd 1 only (i.e., dec every rnd) until 8 (16, 16) sts rem.

FINISHING

Knit the 2 (4, 4) sts from Needle 1 onto Needle 3—4 (8, 8) sts each on 2 needles. Cut yarn leaving a 10" (25.5 cm) tail. Thread tail on a tapestry needle and use the Kitchener st (see Glossary) to graft live sts tog. Weave in loose ends. With yarn threaded on a tapestry needle, tighten up any holes at gussets, if necessary. Block lightly.

Checkerboard Rib Chart

Broken Rib Chart

☐ knit on RS; purl on WS

• purl on RS; knit on WS

☐ pattern repeat

ballet
FLATS

*T*here are lots of patterns for knitted or felted slippers, but **Marta McCall's** knitted ballet flats may be a first. Marta knitted each flat in a single piece from the center of the sole and added intarsia flowers across the toes. She embellished the colorwork with cotton embroidery floss to add a bit of sheen and bound the upper edge with coordinating velvet ribbon to complete the feminine look.

FINISHED SIZE About 8 (9, 10)" (20.5 [23, 25.5] cm) long. To fit women's U.S. shoe size 6–7 (7½–8½, 9–11). Flats shown measure 9" (23 cm) long.

YARN Sportweight (#2 Fine). *Shown here:* Frog Tree 100% Alpaca Wool Type 2204 (100% alpaca; 130 yd [119 m]/50 g): #008 brown, 2 (2, 3) skeins; #31 periwinkle, #20 orange, #28 rose, #46 acid green, and #41 dark green, 1 skein each (all sizes).

NEEDLES Size U.S. size 5 (3.75 mm). Adjust needle size if necessary to obtain the correct gauge.

NOTIONS Markers (m); tapestry needle; sharp-point sewing needle; 1 yd (1 m) ⅝" (1.5 cm) brown velvet ribbon; 6-ply embroidery floss as foll: orange, light green, and dark green, 2 skeins each; brown, yellow, rose, light pink, silver/blue, and light blue, 1 skein each.

GAUGE 21 stitches and 30 rows = 4" (10 cm) in stockinette stitch with yarn doubled.

NOTES

+ Yarn is used doubled throughout.

+ The flats are knitted outward from the center of the sole; both have the same shape.

+ The colorwork areas are worked in the Fair Isle method with the unused yarn stranded across the wrong side and woven in every 3 stitches to prevent long floats.

+ To make the flats slip resistant, add leather or suede soles.

Chart A

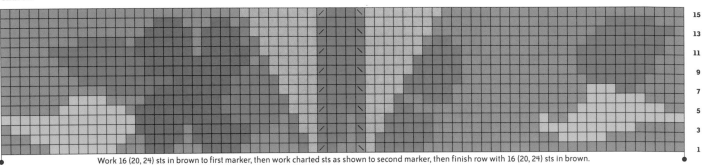

15
13
11
9
7
5
3
1

Work 16 (20, 24) sts in brown to first marker, then work charted sts as shown to second marker, then finish row with 16 (20, 24) sts in brown.

Chart B

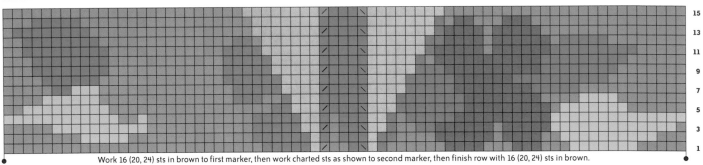

15
13
11
9
7
5
3
1

Work 16 (20, 24) sts in brown to first marker, then work charted sts as shown to second marker, then finish row with 16 (20, 24) sts in brown.

knit on RS; purl on WS

☐ brown

☐ periwinkle

☐ orange

☐ rose

☐ acid green

☐ dark green

☐ no stitch—ignore and work next non-gray st

● marker

☑ k2tog on RS in colors as shown on chart

☑ ssk on RS in colors as shown on chart

FIRST BALLET FLAT

With two strands of brown held tog, CO 68 (76, 84) sts.

Row 1 (WS) K1, M1 (see Glossary), k31 (35, 39), M1, [k1, M1] 4 times, k31 (35, 39), M1, k1—75 (83, 91) sts.

Row 2 and all even-numbered rows (RS) Knit.

Row 3 K1, M1, k34 (38, 42), M1, [k1, M1] 4 times, k35 (39, 43), M1, k1—82 (90, 98).

Row 5 K1, M1, k38 (42, 46), M1, [k1, M1] 4 times, k38 (42, 46), M1, k1—89 (97, 105).

Row 7 K1, M1, k41 (45, 49), M1, [k1, M1] 4 times, k42 (46, 50), M1, k1—96 (104, 112) sts.

Row 9 K1, M1, k45 (49, 53), M1, [k1, M1] 4 times, k45 (49, 53), M1, k1—103 (111, 119) sts.

Row 11 Knit.

Row 12 Change to St st and with brown, k16 (20, 24), place marker (pm), work Row 1 of Chart A, dec as indicated, pm, with brown, k16 (20, 24)—101 (109, 117) sts rem.

Row 13 (WS) With brown, p16 (20, 24) sts to first m, slip marker (sl m), work Row 2 of Chart A to second m, sl m, with brown p16 (20, 24).

Rows 14–26 Cont in St st working 16 (20, 24) sts with brown to first m, then work as charted to second m, work 16 (20, 24) sts with brown—87 (95, 103) sts rem after Row 15 of chart is completed.

Row 27 (WS) With brown, p17 (18, 19), p2tog, [p1, p2tog] 8 (9, 10) times, p1, p2togtbl (see Glossary), [p1, p2tog] 8 (9, 10) times, p17 (18, 19)—69 (75, 81) sts rem.

BO all sts purlwise. Cut yarn, leaving a 40" (101.5 cm) tail.

SECOND BALLET FLAT

Work as for first ballet flat, but substitute Chart B for Chart A.

FINISHING

Note Check out YouTube (search for Marta McCall) for a demonstration of the finishing instructions.

Carefully weave in all loose ends taking care not to create puckers.

Embroidery

Note Double embroidery floss (12 strands total) throughout. With orange embroidery floss threaded on a sharp-point needle, work chain sts (see Glossary) to outline orange flowers. Outline rose flowers with rose chain sts. Outline periwinkle flowers with silver/blue chain sts. Outline acid green leaves with light green chain sts. Outline dark green leaves with dark green chain sts. With yellow, work French knots (see Glossary) in the centers of orange flowers. With light pink, work French knots in centers of rose flowers. With light blue, work French knots in centers of periwinkle flowers.

Seams

With RS facing and 40" (101.5 cm) yarn tail threaded on a tapestry needle, use a whipstitch (see Glossary) to sew heel and bottom of sole, taking care to keep seam as flat as possible.

Ribbon Edging

Starting at the center back of heel, fold velvet ribbon in half over the top edge of flat. With two strands of brown embroidery floss threaded on a sharp-point needle, use tiny ⅛" (3 mm) whipstitches to sew in place. Cut ribbon ½" (1.3 cm) longer than opening and fold excess under to achieve a smooth edge, then sew in place.

animal
CRACKERS

*J*oLene Treace had the good luck to have two new babies added to her extended family in the past year, which led her to design baby sweaters. The adorable sweaters shown here feature a decorative hem, rolled neckline, and intarsia animal motif. By changing the colors and the intarsia motifs (bear, cat, or dog), JoLene gave each sweater its own personality. Knitted out of fine merino yarn on small needles, these sweaters have an heirloom quality that will delight any new mother.

FINISHED SIZE About 20¼ (22¼, 24¼)" (51.5 [56.5, 61.5] cm) chest circumference. To fit 6 (9, 12) months. Sweater shown measures 22¼" (56.5 cm).

YARN Fingering weight (#1 Super Fine).
Shown here: Dale of Norway Baby Ull (100% merino; 181 yd [165 m]/ 50 g): 3 (3, 4) balls main color (MC) and 1 ball contrast color (CC). Bear is shown in #2621 tan (MC) and #0020 cream (CC); cat is shown in #5226 dark lavender (MC) and #5701 pale lavender/blue (CC); dog is shown in #8972 deep olive (MC) and #9436 chartreuse (CC).

NEEDLES *Body, sleeves, and neckband:* size U.S. 2 (2.75 mm): straight, 16" (40 cm) circular (cir), and set of 4 or 5 double-pointed (dpn). *Hem:* size U.S. 1 (2.25 mm): 16" (40 cm) cir or straight. Adjust needle size if necessary to obtain the correct gauge.

NOTIONS Stitch holders; marker (m); tapestry needle.

GAUGE 32 stitches and 47 rows = 4" (10 cm) in spot pattern on larger needles, blocked with moderate stretch.

NOTES
+ A selvedge stitch is worked at each edge to facilitate seaming. Knit the selvedge stitches on right-side rows; purl them on wrong-side rows.

+ Work decreases adjacent to the selvedge stitches; do not include the selvedge stitches in the decreases.

+ Work the animal charts in the intarsia method, using a separate ball or bobbin of yarn for each color block and twisting yarn around each other at color changes to prevent holes from forming.

stitch guide

+ HEM PATTERN

Rows 1, 3, 5, and 7 (RS) Knit with MC.

Rows 2, 4, 6 (WS) Purl with MC.

Row 8 Drop MC, join CC, and purl across.

Row 9 K1 (selvedge st; see Notes), *k2tog, yo; rep from * to last st, k1 (selvedge st).

Row 10 Cut off CC, leaving a 6" (15 cm) tail. Pick up MC and purl across.

Rows 11, 13, and 15 Knit.

Rows 12 and 14 Purl.

Row 16 Cut off MC yarn, leaving a 6" (15 cm) tail. Join CC and purl across.

Row 17 K1, *k2tog; rep from * to last st, k1.

Row 18 With larger needle, p1, *k1, k1 into the strand between the two needles (do not twist the strand) to inc 1 st; rep from * to last st, p1.
Cut off CC, leaving a 6" (15 cm) tail.

+ SPOT PATTERN (multiple of 4 sts)

Rows 1 and 3 (RS) Knit.

Row 2 (WS) Purl.

Row 4 *K1, p3; rep from *.
Repeat Rows 1–4 for pattern.

BACK

With MC, smaller straight needles, and using the knitted method (see Glossary), CO 82 (90, 98) sts. Work 18 rows of hem patt (see Stitch Guide), changing to larger needle for Row 18. Join MC.

Next row (RS) K1, use the backward-loop method (see Glossary) to CO 1 st, knit to end—83 (91, 99) sts.

Set-up row (WS) P1 (selvedge st; see Notes), p2, work Row 4 of spot patt to last 4 sts, k1, p2, p1 (selvedge st).
Maintaining selvedge sts, work Rows 1–4 of spot patt across center 81 (89, 97) sts.

Shape Armholes

Cont in patt, BO 6 (6, 7) sts at beg of next 2 rows—71 (79, 85) sts rem. Cont in patt for 41 (45, 50) more rows, ending with Row 3 (3, 4) of patt.

Shape Neck

Cont in patt, work 21 (23, 24) sts, place next 29 (33, 37) sts on holder for back neck, join a second ball of yarn, work to end—21 (23, 24) sts rem each side. Working each side separately in patt and working the first and last st of each section as a selvedge st, dec 1 st inside selvedge st at each neck edge every RS row 3 times, then work 0 (0, 1) row even, ending with a RS row—18 (20, 21) sts rem each side. Place sts on holders.

FRONT

CO and work as for back until 17 (19, 21) reps of spot patt have been worked, ending with Row 4 (WS) of patt. Mark center 27 sts for intarsia motif.

Next row (RS; Row 1 of spot patt) Work in patt to marked center sts, work Row 1 of desired animal chart over next 27 sts (see Notes), work to end in patt.
Maintaining spot patt each side of marked sts and joining CC when necessary, work Rows 1–4 of chosen animal chart.

Shape Armholes

(RS; Row 5 of chart) Cont in patt, BO 6 (6, 7) sts at beg of next 2 rows—71 (79, 85) sts rem. Cont in patts, work through Row 31 of animal chart, ending with Row 3 of spot patt. Cut off CC, leaving a 4" (10 cm) tail. Cont with MC, work spot patt across all sts for 10 (9, 10) more rows, ending with Row 1 (4, 1) of patt—37 (36, 37) rows in armholes; armholes measure about 3" (7.5 cm).

Shape Neck

(WS) Cont in patt, work 27 (30, 32) sts, place next 17 (19, 21) sts on holder for front neck, join second ball of yarn, work to end—27 (30, 32) sts rem each side. Cont in patt, at each neck edge BO 3 sts once, then BO 2 sts once, then dec 1 st inside selvedge sts every RS row 4 (5, 6) times—18 (20, 21) sts rem each side. Work 0 (2, 8) more row(s) in patt. Place sts on holders.

Bear

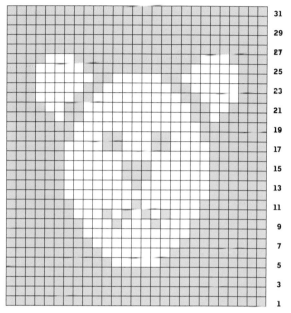

31
29
27
25
23
21
19
17
15
13
11
9
7
5
3
1

Cat

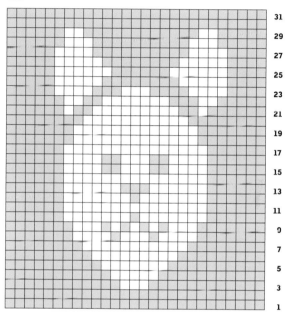

31
29
27
25
23
21
19
17
15
13
11
9
7
5
3
1

□ knit on RS; purl on WS with MC

□ knit on RS; purl on WS with CC

Dog

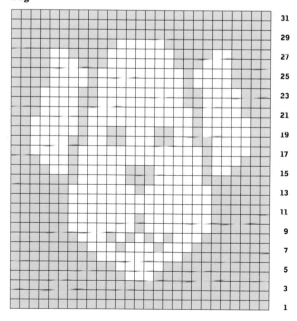

31
29
27
25
23
21
19
17
15
13
11
9
7
5
3
1

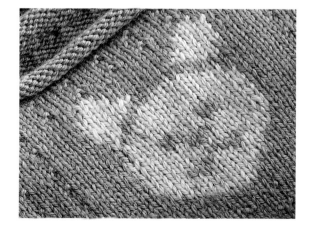

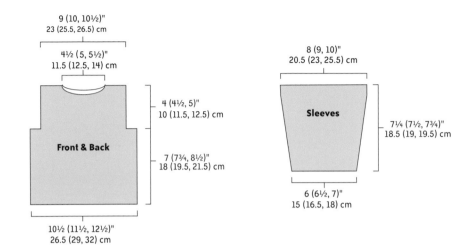

9 (10, 10½)"
23 (25.5, 26.5) cm

4½ (5, 5½)"
11.5 (12.5, 14) cm

4 (4½, 5)"
10 (11.5, 12.5) cm

Front & Back

7 (7¾, 8½)"
18 (19.5, 21.5) cm

10½ (11½, 12½)"
26.5 (29, 32) cm

8 (9, 10)"
20.5 (23, 25.5) cm

Sleeves

7¼ (7½, 7¾)"
18.5 (19, 19.5) cm

6 (6½, 7)"
15 (16.5, 18) cm

SLEEVES

With MC, smaller straight needles, and using the knitted method, CO 48 (52, 56) sts. Working the first and last sts as selvedge sts, work 18 rows of hem patt, changing to larger needles for Row 18.

Next row (RS) K1, M1 (see Glossary), knit to end—49 (53, 57) sts.

Set-up row (WS) P1 (selvedge st), *k1, p3; rep from * to last 4 sts, k1, p2, p1 (selvedge st).

Beg with Row 1, work 2 rows of spot patt.

Inc row (Row 3 of patt) K1, M1, work in patt as established to last st, M1, k1—2 sts inc'd.

Cont in patt, inc 1 st each end of needle (inside selvedge sts) in this manner every 8th row 7 (9, 0) times, then every 6th row 0 (0, 11) times, working new sts in patt—65 (73, 81) sts. Work even in patt until 4-row spot patt has been worked a total of 18 (19, 20) times, ending with a WS row. Work 1 RS row. BO all sts.

FINISHING

Block pieces to measurements. Weave in loose ends.

Seams

Place 18 (20, 21) right front shoulder sts on one dpn and corresponding 18 (20, 21) back shoulder sts on another dpn. Hold needles parallel with RS of facing tog and use the three-needle method (see Glossary) to BO sts tog. With MC threaded on a tapestry needle, sew sleeves into armholes, matching centers of sleeves with shoulder seams. Sew sleeve and side seams.

Neckband

With MC, larger cir needle, RS facing, and beg at left shoulder seam, pick up and knit 14 (17, 20) sts along left neck edge, k17 (19, 21) held front neck sts, pick up and knit 14 (17, 20) sts along right neck edge to shoulder seam, 6 (6, 7) sts along right back neck, k29 (33, 37) held back neck sts, then pick up and knit 6 (6, 7) sts along left back neck—86 (98, 112) sts total. Place marker (pm) and join for working in rnds. Knit 12 rnds, adjusting st count on first rnd if necessary by increasing or decreasing to maintain an evenly rolled neck finish. Using the decrease method (see Glossary), BO all sts.

Block again if desired.

fuzzy slipper SOCKS

*T*hese socks are modeled after ones I knitted for my friend, Katie, to keep her feet warm while she had chemotherapy. After putting them on, Katie asked me to make similar socks for her husband and two sons. The socks are worked from the toe up with a modification of Priscilla Gibson-Robert's infamous short-row heel. Working socks from the toe up is ideal if you have a limited amount of yarn—work the foot to the desired length, then work the leg until the yarn runs out.

FINISHED SIZE About 6½ (7, 8, 9, 10)" (16.5 [18, 20.5, 23, 25.5] cm) foot circumference, 7¼ (8¼, 9, 10¼, 11)" (18.5 [21, 23, 26, 28] cm) foot length from back of heel to tip of toe, and 6 (7, 8, 9, 9½)" (15 [18, 20.5, 23, 24] cm) leg length from base of heel to top of leg. To fit U.S. shoe size children's 9–12, (children's 1–4, women's 5–7/men's 4–6, women's 8–10/men's 7–9, women's 11–14/men's 10–13).

YARN Chunky weight (#5 Bulky). *Shown here:* Caron Bliss (60% acrylic, 40% nylon; 82 yd [75 m]/50 g): 2 (2, 2, 3, 3) balls. Shown in #009 jade, #007 merlot, and #005 copper.

NEEDLES Size U.S. 7 (4.5 mm): set of 4 double-pointed (dpn). Adjust needle size if necessary to obtain the correct gauge.

NOTIONS Marker (m); tapestry needle.

GAUGE 8 stitches and 10 rows = 2" (5 cm) in stockinette stitch, worked in rounds.

NOTE
+ To distinguish the paired stitches from single stitches, stretch the stitches on the needles; the two stitches in each pair will cling to one another.

TOE

Using the Eastern method (see Glossary), CO 8 sts (4 on each of 2 needles). With a third needle, knit the first 2 sts again—2 sts on Needle 1 (half of bottom of foot), 4 sts on Needle 2 (instep), 2 sts on Needle 3 (other half of bottom of foot). Place marker (pm) to denote end of rnd. Rnd begins at center of bottom of foot.

Next rnd (inc rnd) On Needle 1, k1, k1f&b; on Needle 2, k1f&b, k2, k1f&b; on Needle 3, k1f&b, k1—12 sts.

Next rnd (inc rnd) On Needle 1, knit to the last st, k1f&b; on Needle 2, k1f&b, knit to last st, k1f&b; on Needle 3, k1f&b, knit to end—16 sts.

Knit 1 rnd even. Rep the last 2 rnds 2 (3, 4, 5, 6) more times, ending with Needle 2 (i.e., do not work sts on Needle 3 on the last rnd)—24 (28, 32, 36, 40) sts; 6 (7, 8, 9, 10) sts on Needle 1, 12 (14, 16, 18, 20) sts on Needle 2, 6 (7, 8, 9, 10) sts on Needle 3.

FOOT

Work even until piece measures 5¾ (6¾, 7½, 8¼, 9)" (14.5 [17, 19, 21, 23] cm) from CO, or about ¾ (1½, 1½, 2, 2)" (2 [3.8, 3.8, 5, 5] cm) less than desired total length.

HEEL

To facilitate working the heel, rearrange sts so that all bottom-of-foot sts are on the same needle by slipping the sts from Needle 1 onto Needle 3—12 (14, 16, 18, 20) heel sts on one needle; 12 (14, 16, 18, 20) instep sts on the other needle. Next, divide the instep sts equally among 2 needles (6 [7, 8, 9, 10] sts on each needle) to facilitate working back and forth on the heel sts. Work the 12 (14, 16, 18, 20) heel sts back and forth in short-rows in two halves as follows.

First Half

Work 1 less st each row as foll:

Row 1 (RS) Knit to the last st, but do not knit the last st, turn work—1 st unworked.

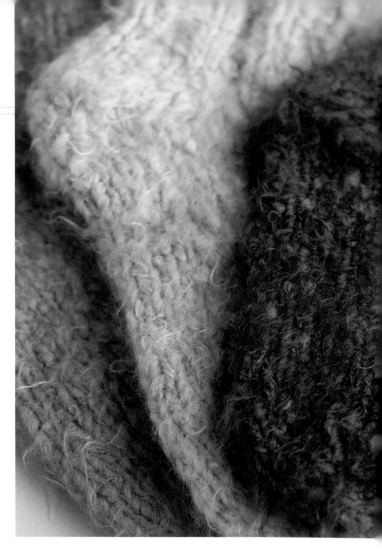

Note Yarnovers are worked at the beg of the foll heel rows to create paired stitches. The yarnover of the pair is worked tog with the adjacent stitch to close the gap at the turning point.

Row 2 (WS) Yo from back to front (this is opposite how yarnovers are usually made; see box at right), purl to the last st but do not purl the last st, turn work—1 st unworked.

Row 3 Yo from front to back as usual, knit to the paired sts at the end of the row, but do not work the paired sts, turn work—3 sts unworked.

Row 4 Yo from back to front, purl to the paired sts at the end of the row, but do not work the paired sts, turn work—3 sts unworked.

Rep Rows 3 and 4, leaving one more paired st at the end of the needle each row until there are 4 (4, 6, 8, 10) unpaired sts at center of row, ending just before the paired sts at the end of a RS row. Do not turn.

Second Half

Cont on the existing RS row, work 1 more st each row as foll:

Row 1 (RS) Knit the first st of the first paired st, k2tog (the yo with the first st of the next pair), turn.

Row 2 (WS) Yo from back to front, purl to the first set of paired sts, purl the first st of the pair, p2tog (the yo with the first st of the next pair), turn.

Row 3 Yo from front to back, knit to the first paired st, knit the first st of the pair (the next 2 sts will be yarnovers), k3tog (the 2 yarnovers with the first st of the next pair), turn.

Row 4 Yo from back to front, purl to the first paired st, purl the first st of the pair (the next 2 sts will be yarnovers), p3tog (the 2 yarnovers with the first st of the next pair), turn.

Rep Rows 3 and 4 until all heel sts have been worked, ending with a WS row—there will be 12 (14, 16, 18, 20) sts plus 1 yo at the beg of the heel needle, which will be used to close the gap between the heel and instep sts.

BACKWARD YARNOVER

Bring the yarn to the back under the needle, then over the top to the front so that the leading leg of the loop is at the back of the needle.

REJOIN FOR WORKING IN ROUNDS

With RS facing, yo from front to back, knit to the yo at the end of the heel needle, transfer this yo to the beg on the next needle (the first needle of the instep sts) and work it tog with the first instep st as k2tog, knit to the last instep st, transfer the yo from the beginning of the heel needle onto the instep needle and work the last instep st tog with the yo as ssk, knit to end of rnd—24 (28, 32, 36, 40) sts total.

Rearrange sts so the 12 (14, 16, 18, 20) instep sts are again on the same needle (Needle 2) and the heel sts are equally divided with 6 (7, 8, 9, 10) sts each on Needle 1 and Needle 3.

ANKLE

Knit 4 (4, 6, 8, 10) rnds even.

LEG

Work k2, p2 rib until piece measures about 6 (7, 8, 9, 9½)" (15 [18, 20.5, 23, 24] cm) from base of heel, or desired total length.

FINISHING

Cut yarn, leaving a tail about 3 times the circumference of the top of the sock. Thread tail on a tapestry needle and use the sewn method (see Glossary) to BO all sts.

Weave in loose ends, tightening the CO sts at the toe and loose sts at the heel short-row turns, if necessary.

alphabet
BLOCKS

*T*ired of the traditional knitted booties, hat, or sweater for a baby gift? Knit something that baby can play with instead—**Kim Hamlin's** soft alternative to traditional wooden alphabet blocks. Kim knitted cotton tubes to fit snuggly around the sides of foam blocks and bright contrasting squares to cover the tops and bottoms. She used a crochet hook to embroider large letters on the sides, then stitched the pieces together.

FINISHED SIZE Each block measures about 3½" (9 cm) wide, 3½" (9 cm) tall, and 3½" (9 cm) deep.

YARN Worsted weight (#4 Medium).
Shown here: Blue Sky Alpacas Dyed Cotton (100% organic cotton; 150 yd [137 m]/100 g): #615 tulip (cream; MC), 2 skeins; #632 Mediterranean (blue), #605 cumin (yellow), #633 pickle (green), and #619 tomato (red), 1 skein each.

NEEDLES Size U.S. 7 (4.5 mm): straight and 12" (30 cm) circular (cir) or set of 4 or 5 double-pointed (dpn). Adjust needle size if necessary to obtain the correct gauge.

NOTIONS Marker (m); tapestry needle, water-soluble marker (available at craft and fabric stores); size F/5 (3.75 mm) crochet hook; seven custom-cut 3½" (9 cm) foam blocks (available online at www.bobsfoam.com).

GAUGE 18 stitches and 22 rows = 4" (10 cm) in stockinette stitch.

BLOCK SIDE
(make 7)

With MC and cir needle or dpn, CO 60 sts. Place marker (pm) and join for knitting in rnds, being careful not to twist sts.

Rnd 1 Knit.

Rnd 2 K7, *sl 1 pwise with yarn in back (wyb), k14; rep from * 2 more times, sl 1 pwise wyb, k7.

Rep these 2 rnds 8 times, then work Rnd 1 once more—19 rnds total; piece measures about 3½" (9 cm) from CO. BO all sts.

TOP/BOTTOM SQUARE
(make 14 in assorted colors)

With desired color, CO 16 sts. Beg and end with a WS row, work even in St st (knit on RS; purl on WS) for a total of 20 rows. BO all sts.

LETTERS

Stretch the block sides around the foam blocks, aligning the slipped sts with the corners of the block. Using water-soluble marker, draw one letter of the alphabet centered in each square, centering the letters so there are three blank sts at each side and four blank rows above and below each letter—six blocks will have four letters each, one block will have two letters only. Remove foam blocks. With a crochet hook and color of your choice, copy each letter with crochet chain-stitch (see Glossary) or the embroidery stitch of your choice. Where necessary, fasten off the yarn and restart in another are to prevent long floats of yarn on the WS of the block.

FINISHING

Weave in loose ends. Stretch the block sides around the foam blocks, aligning slipped sts with corners. With color of your choice threaded on a tapestry needle, use a whipstitch (see Glossary) to join a top and bottom square to each block.

Spritz blocks with lukewarm water to set the sts and dissolve the letter markings.

HEADBAND

The neckband of **Gregory Courtney**'s Herringbone Scarf (page 8) makes a nice pattern on its own. It's modified here as a headband that begins and ends with I-cord ties. This headband is worked with DK weight yarn; try a heavier or lighter yarn (adjusting needle size as necessary) for a wider or narrower band.

CO 3 sts. Work 3-st I-cord (see Glossary) until piece measures 11" (28 cm) from CO.

Next row Working as I-cord, [k1f&b] 3 times —6 sts.

Turn work and with WS facing, [k1f&b] 6 times—12 sts. Cont working back and forth in rows as foll:

Row 1 (RS) [Sl 1 kwise with yarn in back (wyb)] 2 times, knit to last 3 sts, p1 wyb, k1, p1.

Row 2 (WS) Sl 1 kwise wyb, sl 1 pwise with yarn in front (wyf), p1, knit to last 2 sts, sl 1 pwise wyf, p1 through back loop (tbl), p1.

Rep Rows 1 and 2 until piece measures about 13½" (34.5 cm) from last inc row.

Next row (RS) [k2tog] 6 times—6 sts.

Cont working as I-cord (i.e., pull yarn across back of sts and cont with RS still facing), [k2tog] 3 times—3 sts rem. Work 3-st I-cord until piece measures 11" (28 cm) from last dec row. Slip the second and third sts over the first and off the needle—1 st rem. Cut yarn and pull tail through rem st to fasten off.

Weave in loose ends. Block lightly.

FINISHED SIZE About 1½" (3.8 cm) wide and 13½" (34.5 cm) long, excluding 11" (28 cm) strap at each end.

YARN DK weight (#3 Light). *Shown here:* GGH Maxima (100% merino wool; 120 yd [110 m]/50 g): #10 dijon, less than 25 yards.

NEEDLES Size U.S. 5 (3.75 mm): set of 2 double-pointed (dpn). Adjust needle size if necessary to obtain the correct gauge.

NOTIONS Tapestry needle.

GAUGE About 12 stitches and 24 rows = 2" (5 cm) in garter stitch.

fair isle
NAPKIN RINGS

To try out different Fair Isle patterns, **Therese Inverso** knits little tubes that double as napkin rings. Make a coordinating set by using a different color sequence for each ring —you'll learn which colors resonate with each other before embarking on a large project, and you'll end up with a handy gift. Your friends will entertain in style, and should one of these rings roll off the table, it will do so quietly.

FINISHED SIZE About 5½" (14 cm) in circumference and 2½" (6.5 cm) in length, before felting; about 4½" (11.5 cm) in circumference and 2" (5 cm) in length, after felting.

YARN Fingering weight (#1 Super Fine).
Shown here: Jamieson's Shetland Spindrift (100% Shetland wool; 115 yd [105 m]/50 g): #1190 burnt umber (rust), #572 red currant (burgundy), #425 mustard (gold), #365 chartreuse, and #168 Clyde blue, 1 ball each. This is enough to make about 12 napkin rings.

NEEDLES Size U.S. 3 (3.25): set of 4 or 5 double-pointed (dpn). Adjust needle size if necessary to obtain the correct gauge.

NOTIONS Smooth cotton waste yarn for provisional cast-on; tapestry needle; lingerie bag for felting.

GAUGE 28 stitches and 28 rounds = 4" (10 cm) in charted pattern, worked in rounds before felting.

NOTES
+ Cast on and bind off loosely so that the edges roll to the outside (this will form a nice ridge when the piece is felted).

+ Leave 4" (10 cm) tails of yarn when changing colors.

+ Position the Fair Isle pattern so that each needle ends with a complete pattern repeat.

+ To prevent all color-change tails from occurring at the same place, when the pattern calls for a new color to be joined, begin the round with a different needle, thereby shifting the beginning of the round and subsequent color changes.

+ Napkin rings are shown in three different Fair Isle patterns with four different color orders of each and in random stripes of stockinette stitch.

NAPKIN RING

With cotton waste yarn and using the crochet-on provisional method (see Glossary), CO 36 sts. Divide sts evenly onto 3 needles. Leaving a 30" (76 cm) tail, knit these sts with A, then join for working in rnds, being careful not to twist sts. This counts as Rnd 1 of chart. Working the chart and colorway of your choice, work to the end of the chart. Cut off yarn, leaving a 30" (76 cm) tail of A. Thread this tail on a tapestry needle and use the sewn method (see Glossary) to BO all sts. Carefully remove waste yarn from provisional CO and place the exposed sts in the correct orientation on dpns. With A, use the sewn method to BO all sts.

FINISHING

Weave in loose ends.

Felting

Place the napkin ring(s) in a lingerie bag. Follow the instructions for felting the Oven Mitts on page 44. It takes more time to felt small objects—it may take 10 complete cycles to achieve the desired effect. If desired, put the lingerie bag in the washer with normal loads of clothes (do not include it in loads that have bleach). Take the ring(s) out of the bag between cycles and stretch them lengthwise or widthwise as necessary to achieve a pleasing shape.

Arrowhead

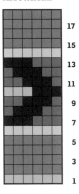

Checkerboard

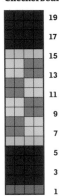

Diamond

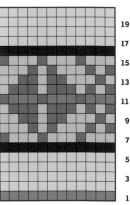

knit each rnd

 burnt umber

red currant

mustard

chartreuse

clyde blue

pattern repeat

ADDITIONAL VARIATIONS

+ To simplify knitting a number of napkin rings, work several in succession in a long tube. CO and BO with A, work the charted pattern and colorway as desired, working 4 rnds of A between each charted repeat. Weave in loose ends. Place the tube in a lingerie bag and felt as described for Oven Mitts on page 44, but when the pieces are about halfway felted and the individual sts are difficult to distinguish, turn the tube inside out and carefully cut between the purl bumps in the center of each 4-rnd separating section of A. Place the cut rings back in the lingerie bag and continue felting. Don't worry about the raw edges—they will get a naturally finished edge during the rest of the felting process (a trick Therese learned from her fiber-artist friend, Nina Mona). The cut edges will achieve a rustic "finish" in the process.

+ For a more refined finish, knit a round with cotton waste yarn between each napkin ring and leave a 30" (76 cm) tail of A at the beg and end of each ring. Before felting, remove the waste yarn and use the tails to use the sewn method to BO the live sts.

+ For a simpler variation, work solid-color stripes instead of a Fair Isle pattern. To avoid weaving in loose ends, make a "magic ball" by wet-splicing (see page 44) 2 yd (1.8 meter) lengths of colors tog before knitting. If desired, personalize the felted rings with embroidered flowers or initials before or after they've been felted.

felted mohair
SCARVES

hat can you do with a skein of yarn? **Mags Kandis** knits a strip from a ball of mohair-silk-blend yarn, felts it in a basin, pulls it into an interesting shape, then adds a little embroidery, and has a one-of-a kind gift. To allow for felting, Mags intentionally works the yarn at a looser gauge than specified on the ball band. Unlike felted wool, these mohair-silk scarves are soft and whisper light.

FINISHED SIZE About 4½" (11.5 cm) wide and 38" (96.5 cm) long, measured from point to point, after felting.

YARN Fingering weight (#1 Super Fine).
Shown here: Rowan Kidsilk Haze (70% super kid mohair; 30% silk; 229 yd [210 m]/25 g): 1 ball. Shown in #597 jelly (green) and #583 blushes (dark pink).

NEEDLES Size U.S. 7 (4.5 mm): straight. Adjust needle size if necessary to obtain the correct gauge.

NOTIONS Tapestry needle; embroidery needle; DMC 25 Embroidery Cotton in #920 (orange) and #783 (gold), one (8.7 yd [8 m]) skein each; rubber gloves.

GAUGE 19 stitches and 25 rows = 4" (10 cm) in stockinette stitch, before felting.

SCARF

CO 44 sts. Work even in St st until about 36" (91.5 cm) of yarn rem—piece should measure about 45" (114 cm) from CO. Loosely BO all sts.

FINISHING

Weave in loose ends.

Felting

Fill one basin with hot, soapy water (a quarter-size squish of baby shampoo is enough) and another basin with ice water (with ice cubes). Agitate and rub the scarf in the hot water (wear gloves), then transfer it to the ice water. Rep back and forth between the two (add hot and cold water as needed to maintain the temperature difference) until the pieces have felted and the individual stitches become obscure and the piece has shrunk to the desired size. Pull the ends and shape the scarf as desired. Lay flat to air-dry completely. Gently press with a cool iron, if desired.

Stitching

With orange embroidery cotton (for green scarf) or gold embroidery cotton (for dark pink scarf) threaded on a tapestry needle, work running stitches or backstitches (see Glossary) in free-form patt as desired.

FELTED HOT PADS

Knit two hot pads at once by using a provisional cast-on, knitting for the desired length, then using an I-cord bind-off to finish off the live stitches. Midway through the felting process, cut the tube in half. The cut edges will be "finished" during the rest of the felting.

With smooth cotton waste yarn, 24" (60 cm) cir needle, and using the crochet-on method (see Glossary), provisionally CO 88 sts. Leaving a 6" (15 cm) tail, knit the sts with desired color, then join for working in rnds, being careful not to twist sts. Knit 1 rnd. Cont as foll, changing colors for stripes as desired:

Rnd 1 *K2, p2; rep from *.
Rnd 2 Knit.

Rep these 2 rnds 5 more times—12 rnds total. Knit every rnd until piece measures about 10" (25.5 cm) from CO. Rep Rnds 1 and 2 of rib 6 times—12 rnds total. Knit 2 rnds even

With desired color and larger dpn, CO 3 sts. Work I-cord BO as for Oven Mitts on page 44, adding a 7" (18 cm) I-cord loop. Remove waste yarn from provisional CO and place live sts in the correct orientation on cir needle. Work I-cord BO as before, working another 7" (10 cm) loop at the opposite corner.

Felt as for Oven Mitts on page 44, but when the piece is about halfway felted, cut the two sides apart. The cut edges will be "finished" during the rest of the felting. Gently tug the pieces into shape along the way. Trim loose fibers.

FINISHED SIZE Two hot pads, each about 5¾" (14.5 cm) wide and 5¾" (14.5 cm) tall, after felting.

YARN Worsted weight (#4 Medium).
Shown here: Schoolhouse Press Unspun Icelandic Wool (100% Icelandic wool; 300 yd [274 m]/3½ oz): less than 1 wheel each of MC and CC. Shown in gold (MC) and brown (CC).

NEEDLES *Pad:* size U.S. 6 (4 mm): 24" (60 cm) circular (cir), 16" (40 cm) cir, and set of 5 double-pointed (dpn). *I-cord edging:* size U.S. 7 (4.5 mm): set of 2 dpn. Adjust needle size if necessary to obtain the correct gauge.

NOTIONS Smooth cotton waste yarn for provisional CO; markers (m); tapestry needle.

GAUGE 20 stitches = 4" (10 cm) in stockinette stitch on smaller needles, worked in rounds. Row gauge is not important.

cable & twist
PILLOW

*P*illows make nice housewarming gifts—there's always room for one more. And **Vicki Square's** cable pillow is so simple, you'll want to make several. Just knit a rectangle with a few buttonholes in the ribbing at one end, a simple cable pattern in the center, and a bit of ribbing at the other end. Fold each short end of the rectangle to the center, sew it together, insert a pillow form, button it closed, and you're done! The subtle striations in the hand-dyed yarn shown here add interesting color depth.

FINISHED SIZE About 16" (40.5 cm) square.

YARN Chunky weight (#5 Bulky). *Shown here:* Fiesta Yarns Kokopelli (60% mohair, 40% wool; 125 yd [118 m]/100 g): #3007 cajeta, 3 skeins.

NEEDLES Size U.S. 9 (5.5 mm). Adjust needle size if necessary to obtain the correct gauge.

NOTIONS Tapestry needle; three 1¼" (3.2 cm) buttons; 16" (40.5 cm) pillow form; size J/10 (6 mm) crochet hook.

GAUGE 15½ stitches and 20 rows = 4" (10 cm) in stockinette stitch; 14 stitches and 20 rows = 4" (10 cm) in pattern stitch, stretched.

stitch guide

+ LT (Left Twist; worked over 2 sts)
Knit into the back of the second st on the left needle, then knit into the front of the first st, then slip both sts off the needle.

+ 3/3RC (worked over 6 sts)
Slip 3 sts onto cable needle and hold in back of work, k3, k3 from cable needle.

PILLOW

CO 49 sts.

Set-up row (WS) *K1, p1; rep from * to last st, k1.

Work in single rib as foll:

Row 1 (RS): P1, *k1, p1; rep from *.

Row 2 (WS) K1, *p1, k1; rep from *.

Rep these 2 rows once more.

Buttonhole row (RS) Keeping in rib as established, work 12 sts, [yo, k2tog, work 10 sts] 2 times, yo, k2tog, work 11 sts—3 buttonholes.

Work 2 rows in rib as established.

Next row (WS) Work in rib and *at the same time* inc 10 sts evenly spaced—59 sts.

Work cable patt as foll:

Row 1 [P2, k3, p2, k6] 4 times, p2, k3, p2.

Rows 2, 4, and 6 K2, p3, k2, *p6, k2, p3, k2; rep from *.

Row 3 [P2, LT (see Stitch Guide), k1, p2, 3/3RC (see Stitch Guide)] 4 times, p2, LT, k1, p2.

Row 5 Rep Row 1.

Row 7 [P2, k1, LT, p2, k6] 4 times, p2, k1, LT, p2.

Row 8 K2, p3, k2, *p6, k2, p3, k2; rep from *.

Rep Rows 1–8 until piece measures about 32" (81.5 cm) from CO, ending with Row 3 of patt.

Next row (WS) Dec 10 sts as foll: [k2tog, p3, k2tog, p6] 4 times, k2tog, p3, k2tog—49 sts rem.

Work in single rib as foll:

Row 1 (RS) P1, *k1, p1; rep from *.

Row 2 (WS) K1, *p1, k1; rep from *.

Rep the last 2 rows two more times, then work Row 1 once more. With WS facing, BO all sts in patt.

FINISHING

Lay knitted piece flat with RS facing up. Mark midpoint on each long (selvedge) edge. With RS tog, fold the buttonhole edge to the middle, aligning the buttonholes at the marked point. Fold the opposite short edge to the middle, completely overlapping the bands of ribbing and pin in place. With yarn and a crochet hook, work a slip-stitch seam (see Glossary) along each side, working through all three layers at the ribbing. To set the seams, place a rolled up hand towel inside the pillow, directly under a seam. Steam the seam, being careful not to touch the iron to the knitted fabric. Finger-press the seam to reduce some of the bulk.

Turn pillow right side out. Sew buttons to ribbing, opposite buttonholes. Insert pillow form. Fasten buttons.

abbreviations

beg(s)	begin(s); beginning
BO	bind off
CC	contrasting color
cm	centimeter(s)
cn	cable needle
CO	cast on
cont	continue(s); continuing
dec(s)	decrease(s); decreasing
dpn	double-pointed needles
foll	follow(s); following
g	gram(s)
inc(s)	increase(s); increasing
k	knit
k1f&b	knit into the front and back of same stitch
kwise	knitwise, as if to knit
m	marker(s)
MC	main color
mm	millimeter(s)
M1	make one (increase)
p	purl
p1f&b	purl into front and back of same stitch
patt(s)	pattern(s)
psso	pass slipped stitch over
pwise	purlwise, as if to purl
rem	remain(s); remaining

rep	repeat(s); repeating
rev St st	reverse stockinette stitch
rnd(s)	round(s)
RS	right side
sl	slip
sl st	slip st (slip 1 stitch purlwise unless otherwise indicated)
ssk	slip 2 stitches knitwise, one at a time, from the left needle to right needle, insert left needle tip through both front loops and knit together from this position (1 stitch decrease)
st(s)	stitch(es)
St st	stockinette stitch
tbl	through back loop
tog	together
WS	wrong side
wyb	with yarn in back
wyf	with yarn in front
yd	yard(s)
yo	yarnover
*	repeat starting point
**	repeat all instructions between asterisks
( )	alternate measurements and/or instructions
[ ]	work instructions as a group a specified number of times

glossary

BIND-OFFS
Decrease Bind-Off

Working very loosely to prevent the bind-off edge from becoming too tight, *k2tog **(Figure 1)**, then slip this stitch onto the left needle tip without twisting it **(Figure 2)**. Repeat from * for the desired number of stitches.

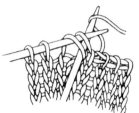 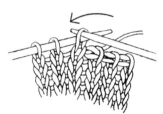

Figure 1   Figure 2

Sewn Bind-Off

Cut yarn three times the width of the knitting to be bound off and thread onto a tapestry needle. Working from right to left, *insert tapestry needle purlwise (from right to left) through the first two stitches **(Figure 1)** and pull the yarn through. Bring tapestry needle knitwise (from left to right) through first stitch **(Figure 2)**, pull yarn through, and slip this stitch off the knitting needle. Repeat from * for desired number of stitches.

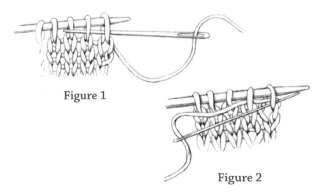

Figure 1

Figure 2

Three-Needle Bind-Off

Place the stitches to be joined onto two separate needles and hold the needles parallel so that the right sides of knitting face together. Insert a third needle into the first stitch on each of two needles **(Figure 1)** and knit them together as one stitch **(Figure 2)**, *knit the next stitch on each needle the same way, then use the left needle tip to lift the first stitch over the second and off the needle **(Figure 3)**. Repeat from * until no stitches remain on first two needles. Cut yarn and pull tail through last stitch to secure.

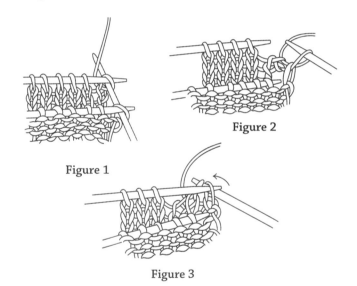

Figure 1

Figure 2

Figure 3

CAST-ONS
Backward-Loop Cast-On

*Loop working yarn and place it on needle backward so that it doesn't unwind. Repeat from *.

Cable Cast-On

If there are no stitches on the needles, make a slipknot of working yarn and place it on the needle, then use the knitted method to cast-on one more stitch—2 stitches on needle. Hold needle with working yarn in your left hand with the wrong side of the work facing you. *Insert right needle *between* the first two stitches on left needle (**Figure 1**), wrap yarn around needle as if to knit, draw yarn through (**Figure 2**), and place new loop on left needle (**Figure 3**) to form a new stitch. Repeat from * for the desired number of stitches, always working between the first two stitches on the left needle.

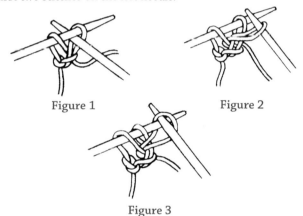

Figure 1   Figure 2

Figure 3

Crochet-On Cast-On

Place a slipknot on a crochet hook. Hold the needle and yarn in your left hand with the yarn under the needle. Place hook over needle, wrap yarn around hook, and pull the loop through the slipknot (**Figure 1**). *Bring yarn to back under needle, wrap yarn around hook, and pull it through loop on hook (**Figure 2**). Repeat from * until there is one less than the desired number of stitches. Bring the yarn to the back and slip the remaining loop from the hook onto the needle.

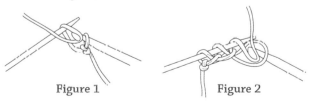

Figure 1   Figure 2

Knitted Cast-On

Make a slipknot of working yarn and place it on the left needle if there are no stitches already there. *Use the right needle to knit the first stitch (or slipknot) on left needle (**Figure 1**) and place new loop onto left needle to form a new stitch (**Figure 2**). Repeat from * for the desired number of stitches, always working into the last stitch made.

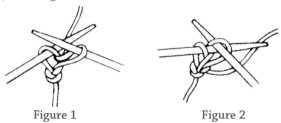

Figure 1   Figure 2

Long-Tail (Continental) Cast-On

Hold two dpn parallel to each other. Leaving a 4" (10cm) tail hanging to the front between the two needles, wrap the yarn around both needles from back to front, then bring the yarn forward between the needles (**Figure 1**). Use a third dpn to knit across the loops on the top needle (**Figure 2**). With RS facing, rotate the two needles so that the bottom needle is on the top. Knit across the loopsw on the new top needle (**Figure 3**). There will be four stitches on two needles (**Figure 4**).

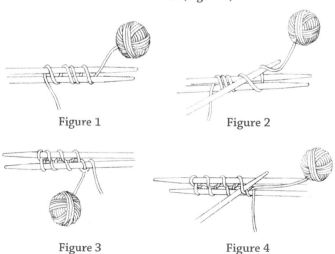

Figure 1   Figure 2

Figure 3   Figure 4

CROCHET
Crochet Chain (ch)
Make a slipknot and place it on crochet hook if there isn't a loop already on the hook. *Yarn over hook and draw through loop on hook. Repeat from * for the desired number of stitches. To fasten off, cut yarn and draw end through last loop formed.

Single Crochet (sc)
*Insert hook into the second chain from the hook (or the next stitch), yarn over hook and draw through a loop, yarn over hook (Figure 1), and draw it through both loops on hook (Figure 2). Repeat from * for the desired number of stitches.

Figure 1   Figure 2

Slip-Stitch Crochet (sl st)
*Insert hook into stitch, yarn over hook and draw a loop through both the stitch and the loop already on hook. Repeat from * for the desired number of stitches.

Purl 2 Together Through Back Loops (p2togtbl)
Bring right needle tip behind two stitches on left needle, enter through the back loop of the second stitch, then the first stitch, then purl them together.

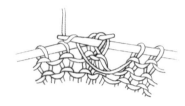

Slip, Slip, Knit (ssk)
Slip two stitches individually knitwise (Figure 1), insert left needle tip into the front of these two slipped stitches, and use the right needle to knit them together through their back loops (Figure 2).

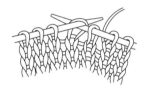 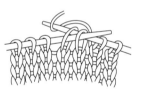

Figure 1   Figure 2

EMBROIDERY
Backstitch
Bring threaded needle out from back to front between the first two knitted stitches you want to cover. *Insert the needle at the right edge of the right stitch to be covered, then bring it back out at the left edge of the second stitch. Insert the needle again between these two stitches and bring it out between the next two to be covered. Repeat from *.

Chain Stitch

Bring threaded needle out from back to front, form a short loop, then insert needle back in where it came out. Keeping the loop under the needle, bring the needle back out a short distance to the right.

Crochet Chain Stitch

Holding the yarn under the background, insert crochet hook through the center of a knitted stitch, pull up a loop, insert hook into the center of the next stitch to the right, pull up a second loop through the first loop on the hook. Repeat from *.

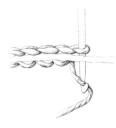

Duplicate Stitch

Bring threaded needle out from back to front at the base of the V of the knitted stitch you want to cover. *Working right to left, pass needle in and out under the stitch in the row above it and back into the base of the same stitch. Bring needle back out at the base of the V of the next stitch to the left. Repeat from * for desired number of stitches.

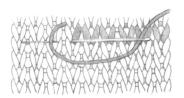

French Knot

Bring threaded needle out of knitted background from back to front, wrap yarn around needle one to three times, and use your thumb to hold the wraps in place while you insert needle into background a short distance from where it came out. Pull the needle through the wraps into the background.

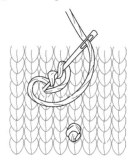

Running Stitch

Bring threaded needle in and out of background to form a dashed line.

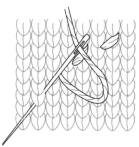

GRAFTING
Kitchener Stitch

Arrange stitches on two needles so that there is the same number of stitches on each needle. Hold the needles parallel to each other with wrong sides of the knitting together. Allowing about ½" (1.3 cm) per stitch to be grafted, thread matching yarn on a tapestry needle. Work from right to left as follows:

Step 1 Bring tapestry needle through the first stitch on the front needle as if to purl and leave the stitch on the needle (**Figure 1**).

Step 2 Bring tapestry needle through the first stitch on the back needle as if to knit and leave that stitch on the needle (**Figure 2**).

Step 3 Bring tapestry needle through the first front stitch as if to knit and slip this stitch off the needle, then bring tapestry needle through the next front stitch as if to purl and leave this stitch on the needle (**Figure 3**).

Step 4 Bring tapestry needle through the first back stitch as if to purl and slip this stitch off the needle, then bring tapestry needle through the next back stitch as if to knit and leave this stitch on the needle (**Figure 4**).

Repeat Steps 3 and 4 until one stitch remains on each needle, adjusting the tension to match the rest of the knitting as you go. To finish, bring tapestry needle through the front stitch as if to knit and slip this stitch off the needle, then bring tapestry needle through the back stitch as if to purl and slip this stitch off the needle.

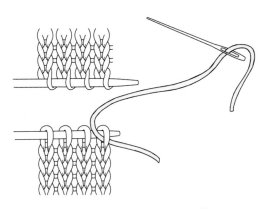

Figure 1

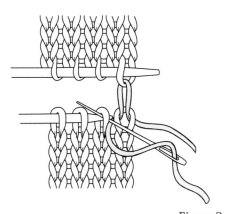

Figure 3

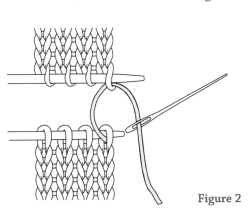

Figure 2

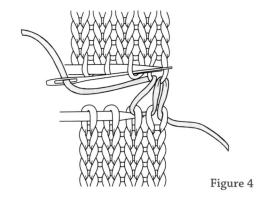

Figure 4

I-Cord (also called Knit-Cord)

Using two double-pointed needles, cast on the desired number of stitches (usually three to four). Knit these stitches, then *without turning the work, slide stitches to other end of needle, pull the yarn around the back, and knit the stitches as usual. Repeat from * for desired length.

INCREASES
Bar Increase (k1f&b)

Knit into a stitch but leave it on the left needle (**Figure 1**), then knit through the back loop of the same stitch (**Figure 2**) and slip the original stitch off the needle (**Figure 3**).

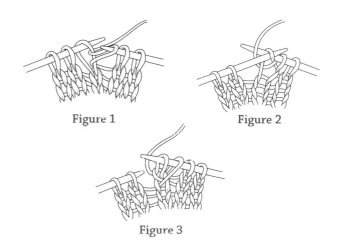

Figure 1   Figure 2

Figure 3

Raised Make-One—Left Slant (M1L)

Note Use the left slant if no direction of slant is specified. With left needle tip, lift the strand between the last knitted stitch and the first stitch on the left needle from front to back (**Figure 1**), then knit the lifted loop through the back (**Figure 2**).

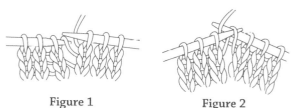

Figure 1   Figure 2

Raised Make-One—Right Slant (M1R)

With left needle tip, lift the strand between the needles from back to front (**Figure 1**). Knit the lifted loop through the front (**Figure 2**).

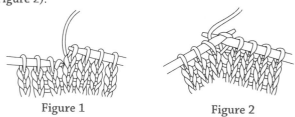

Figure 1   Figure 2

PICK UP AND PURL

With wrong side of work facing and working from right to left, *insert needle tip under selvedge stitch from the far side to the near side, wrap yarn around needle (**Figure 1**), and pull a loop through (**Figure 2**). Repeat from * for desired number of stitches.

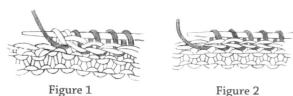

Figure 1   Figure 2

SEAMS
Backstitch Seam

Pin pieces to be seamed with right sides facing together. Working from right to left into the edge stitch, bring threaded needle up between the next two stitches on each piece of knitted fabric, then back down through both layers, one stitch to the right of the starting point (Figure 1). *Bring the needle up through both layers a stitch to the left of the backstitch just made (Figure 2), then back down to the right, through the same hole used before (Figure 3). Repeat from *, working backward one stitch for every two stitches worked forward.

Blanket Stitch

Hold together the pieces to be seamed. Working into the edge stitch of each piece, *bring tip of threaded needle in and out of a knitted stitch, place working yarn under needle tip, then bring threaded needle through the stitch and tighten. Repeat from *, always bringing threaded needle on top of working yarn.

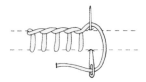

Fishbone Stitch

Place the pieces to be seamed on a table, right sides facing up. Anchor the tail of the seaming yarn to one piece. Beginning on the right side of the seam, *insert tapestry needle under one-half selvedge stitch from back to front, then insert needle under one-half selvedge stitch directly opposite on the left side of the seam, under the head of the newly made stitch. Gently pull the working yarn to pull the sides together. Repeat from * for each stitch.

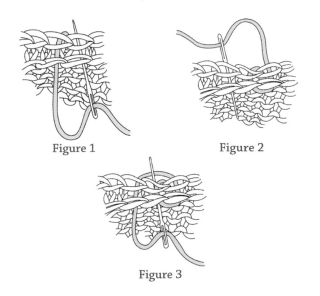

Figure 1   Figure 2

Figure 3

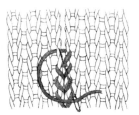

Slip-Stitch Crochet Seam

With right sides together and working one stitch at a time, *insert crochet hook through both thicknesses into the stitch just below the bound-off edge (or one stitch in from the selvedge edge), grab a loop of yarn (**Figure 1**), and draw this loop through both thicknesses, then through the loop on the hook (**Figure 2**). Repeat from *, keeping even tension on the crochet stitches.

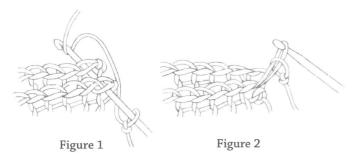

Figure 1   Figure 2

Whipstitch

Hold pieces to be sewn together so that the edges to be seamed are even with each other. With yarn threaded on a tapestry needle, *insert needle through both layers from back to front, then bring needle to back. Repeat from *, keeping even tension on the seaming yarn.

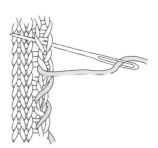

Zipper

With right side facing and zipper closed, pin zipper to the knitted pieces so edges cover the zipper teeth. With contrasting thread and right side facing, baste zipper in place close to teeth (**Figure 1**). Turn work over and with matching sewing thread and needle, stitch outer edges of zipper to wrong side of knitting (**Figure 2**), being careful to follow a single column of stitches in the knitting to keep zipper straight. Turn work back to right side facing, and with matching sewing thread, sew knitted fabric close to teeth (**Figure 3**). Remove basting.

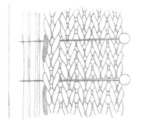 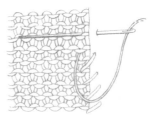

Figure 1   Figure 2

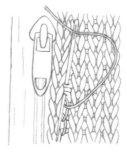

Figure 3

sources for yarn

Blue Sky Alpacas Inc.
PO Box 88
Cedar, MN 55011
blueskyalpacas.com

Brown Sheep Company
100662 County Rd. 16
Mitchell, NE 69357
brownsheep.com

Caron International
PO Box 222
Washington, NC 27889
caron.com

Classic Elite Yarns
122 Western Ave.
Lowell, MA 01851
classiceliteyarns.com

Crystal Palace Yarns
160 23rd St.
Richmond, CA 94804
straw.com/cpy

Dale of Norway
N16 W23390 Stone Ridge Dr.,
Ste. A
Waukesha, WI 53188
dale.no

Diamond Yarn
9697 St. Laurent, Ste. 101
Montreal, QC
Canada H3L 2N1
+
155 Martin Ross, Unit 3
Toronto, ON
Canada M3J 2L9
diamondyarn.com

Universal Yarns/Fibra Natura
284 Ann St.
Concord, NC 28025
universalyarn.com

Fiesta Yarns
4583 Corrales Rd.
Corrales, NM 87048
fiestayarns.com

T&C Imports/Frog Tree Yarns
PO Box 1119
East Dennis, MA 02641
frogtreeyarns.com

Lily
320 Livingstone Ave. S.
Listowel, ON N4W 3H3
sugarncream.com

Lorna's Laces
4229 North Honore St.
Chicago, IL 60613
lornaslaces.net

Louet North America
808 Commerce Park Dr.
Odgensburg, NY 13669
louet.com
in Canada:
3425 Hands Rd.
Prescott, ON
Canada K0E 1T0

Morehouse Farm
141 Milan Hill Rd.
Milan, NY 12571
morehousefarm.com

Muench Yarns
1323 Scott St.
Petaluma, CA 94954
muenchyarns.com
in Canada: Oberlyn Yarns

Oberlyn Yarns
5640 Rue Valcourt
Brossard, QC
Canada J4W 1C5
oberlyn.ca

Plymouth Yarn Co.
500 Lafayette St.
Bristol, PA 19007
plymouthyarn.com

Schoolhouse Press
6899 Cary Bluff
Pittsville, WI 54466
schoolhousepress.com

**Tahki/Stacy Charles Inc./
Filatura Di Crosa**
70–30 80th St., Bldg 36
Ridgewood, NY 11385
tahkistacycharles.com
in Canada: Diamond Yarn

Toots LeBlanc and Co.
tootsleblanc.com
(503) 357-5647

Trendsetter Yarns
16745 Saticoy St., Ste. 101
Van Nuys, CA 91406
trendsetteryarns.com

Tutto Santa Fe
137 West Water St., Ste. 220
Santa Fe, NM 87501
tuttosantafe.com

**Westminster Fibers/
Nashua/Rowan**
165 Ledge St.
Nashua, NH 03060
westminsterfibers.com
In Canada: Diamond Yarn

contributing designers

PAM ALLEN is the creative director for Classic Elite Yarns and the former editor in chief of *Interweave Knits*. She's the author of *Knitting for Dummies* and *Scarf Style*, and coauthor of *Wrap Style, Lace Style, Bag Style,* and *Color Style*.

VÉRONIK AVERY is the author of *Knitting Classic Style* as well as the founding co-owner of St-Denis Yarns. She lives in Montréal, Québec.

NANCY BUSH is the author of *Folk Socks, Folk Knitting in Estonia, Knitting on the Road, Knitting Vintage Socks,* and *Knitted Lace of Estonia*. She is also owner of The Wooly West, a mail-order knitting shop (www.woolywest.com) in Salt Lake City, Utah.

A passionate knitter for nearly thirty years and currently battling an addiction to sock knitting, **GREGORY COURTNEY** has worked as a pattern editor, garment designer, graphic artist, trade show roadie, and stock boy. He can be found most days at Tutto, a knitting store in Santa Fe, and on Ravelry as SirCabelot.

CHRISSY GARDINER designs knitwear and tries to keep up with her two small children in Portland, Oregon. You can find more of her work at gardineryarnworks.com.

KIM HAMLIN lives in Brooklyn, New York, and is a designer, modern dancer, and all-around maker. She is author of *Posh Pooches* and has contributed designs to several books. Visit her blog at inspiredliving-keepitmoving.blogspot.com.

THERESE INVERSO started out teaching music and sewing patchwork quilts, but after reading Elizabeth Zimmermann's *Knitting Without Tears,* she turned to teaching knitting and sewing with felted wool. Most of Therese's designs use techniques "unvented" by Elizabeth Zimmermann and Meg Swanson.

In 1992, **MAGS KANDIS** co-founded Mission Falls where she also served as creative director until 2006. Now she spends her time as a design contributor to major knitting magazine and book publishers. Mags is the author of numerous knitting books, including *Folk Style*. She lives in Ontario, Canada. Visit her website at magskandis.com.

CECILY GLOWIK MACDONALD has a BFA in painting, but knitting is her passion. She has been designing handknits for just five years and has had numerous designs featured in books, magazines, and *Classic Elite Yarns* collections.

MARTA MCCALL is passionate about merging varied craft techniques with knitting. She designs for knitting magazines and yarn companies and publishes her modern and innovative knitwear patterns through her online company, TinkkniT.com. Visit her on Ravelry under MartaMcCall.

KATHY MERRICK designs knitting and crocheting patterns. She lives in Lansdale, Pennsylvania, surrounded by an alarming number of skeins of Koigu and other pretty yarns. She considers this "cheap art," and it makes her happy.

KRISTIN NICHOLAS is a knitwear and stitchery author and designer. She lives in western Massachusetts with her husband and daughter, along with sheep, pigs, chickens, border collies, and farm cats. Visit her website at kristinnicholas.com.

RUTHIE NUSSBAUM learned to knit as a teenager from her grandmother. She now lives in New York City, where she's a reading teacher, knitting instructor, and burgeoning knitwear designer. See more of her work at ruthieknits.com.

VICKI SQUARE is the author of several books, including *The Knitter's Companion, Folk Bags, Folk Hats,* and *Knit Kimono* from Interweave. She lives in Fort Collins, Colorado, where she has a love for yarn and books.

JAYA SRIKRISHNAN is an accomplished designer and teacher who loves to share her expertise and enthusiasm with other knitters. Her designs have been published in several magazines and books.

ELISSA SUGISHITA is an avid knitter and crocheter and has been knitting since she was a little girl. She has a background in the children's clothing industry and aspires to be a clothing designer. She currently works as a computer technician in a major New York publishing company.

JUDITH L. SWARTZ is the author of *Dogs in Knits, Hip to Knit, Hip to Crochet,* and *Getting Started Crochet*. She lives in Spring Green, Wisconsin, where she and her husband are fourth-generation owners of a small department store with, of course, an extensive yarn department.

KATHY TICHO is the owner of Knitche, a fiber and coffee lover's oasis in the western Chicago suburb of Downers Grove.

JOLENE TREACH is a professional member of the Association of Knitwear Designers. JoLene has had designs in a number of publications and also self publishes pattern leaflets through her business, Kristmen's Design Studio.

KATHY ZIMMERMAN is owner of Kathy's Kreations in Ligonier, Pennsylvania, where her customers have dubbed her The Cable Queen. Kathy is a longtime knitwear designer and has had designs published in most major knitting magazines and many knitting books.

index